£2-50   10th March, 2001

To David,

Hope you enjoy a   of the
beauty that is In

              so

              Sinéad xxx

G000041724

SHORT WALKS
IN IRELAND

20 SUPERB WALKING ROUTES
VISITING PLACES OF INTEREST
FROM WICKLOW TO CONNEMARA

SHORT WALKS IN IRELAND

20 SUPERB WALKING ROUTES VISITING PLACES OF INTEREST
FROM WICKLOW TO CONNEMARA

TOM LAWTON

PHOTOGRAPHS BY THE AUTHOR
DIAGRAMS BY DR WILLIAM ROUSE

Gill & Macmillan

This book is dedicated to the beauty of
Ireland and to the friendliness of the people
who live there.

Gill & Macmillan Ltd
Hume Avenue, Park West, Dublin 12
with associated companies throughout the world
www.gillmacmillan.ie
© Tom Lawton 2000
0 7171 3066 5
Diagrams by Dr William Rouse
Design and print origination by Design Image, Dublin
Printed and bound by ColourBooks Ltd, Dublin

A catalogue record for this book is available from
the British Library.

Maps based on Ordnance Survey Ireland
by permission of the Government
(Permit No. 7155)

Jacket Photographs
front: Knockanaffrin Ridge, Comeragh Mountains, Co Waterford
back (top left): Coumshingaun Lough, Comeragh Mountains, Co Waterford
back (top right): Powerscourt Waterfall, Co Wicklow
back (below): Glennahoo Valley, Dingle Peninsula, Co Kerry

CONTENTS

INTRODUCTION

'See one promontory, one mountain, one sea, one river, and see all.'
Socrates (470–399 B.C.)

Ireland is a land blessed with an abundance of wonderful unspoilt countryside. Geological evolution has arranged much of this in the shape of untamed mountainous landscapes, either along or near to the island's magnificent indented coastline. These mountain areas of outstanding natural beauty are perfect for walking across, and the lower parts of these, such as their foothills, and the valleys, forests and woodlands with their lakes and streams that protrude into the higher terrain, make ideal stomping grounds for those keen on undertaking short walks.

Located within this walker's paradise, in addition to the superb scenery, is a wide range of visitor attractions. Many of these places of interest are associated with the great outdoors, and as such they will have special appeal to those who enjoy exercising their legs on short walks. These 'outdoor' attractions include forest parks, heritage and nature trails, historic houses and gardens, castles, bog villages, archaeological and monastic sites, interpretative centres, aquariums, funparks, boating activities and the like.

These magical lands and their contents are, therefore, the compelling reasons for this collection of short walks to associated places of interest. Two additional justifications, should these be needed, are: (1) following the success of my first guidebook on this country, *Walking Ireland*, and based upon the favourable reception of the sequence previously established by my series of guidebooks on the English Lake and Peak Districts, such a book of short walks was the obvious next choice; and (2) walking is correctly regarded as one of the healthiest of exercises and if undertaken regularly it will make a significant contribution to both physical and mental fitness. This 'feel good factor' attached to walking comes through just escaping on regular occasions from the pressures of modern life, enjoying being at one with nature and obtaining fulfilment from successfully completing something that is a challenge appropriate to one's abilities.

Happily, by their very nature short walks may be enjoyed by the widest range of participants, and the diverse opportunities available to exercise in this way may be pursued by people of all ages, of most shapes and sizes, and at virtually any starting level of fitness. Additionally, in the case of the short walks described in this book, only relatively modest periods of time need to be set aside to undertake an enjoyable exercise that is also inherently good for you.

The landscapes amongst which you are invited to exercise your leg muscles in this book include the granite domes of the Wicklow Mountains, the green and pleasant lands of the Nire Valley together with the nearby Comeragh and Knockmealdown Mountains, the ranging seascapes and mountainous terrain of the far south-western peninsulas of Beara, Iveragh and Dingle, the delights of the Killarney National Park, and the awesome, pointed quartzite peaks of Connemara and Mayo. The 20 short walks that will enable you to explore all these fantastic regions in some depth vary greatly in terms of physical demand. At one extreme there are gentle lowland routes, some of which thread around parts of tranquil loughs or follow meandering streams through woodlands along well-defined ways, whilst at the other extreme there are energetic climbs to the tops of moderate hills, sometimes across stretches of rough ground where the route is not always all that clearly marked. These more demanding routes are intended to give those to whom this type of walking appeals a taste of what more adventurous forays into the higher mountains are like and perhaps even generate a healthy appetite for more.

Much of the land that you will walk across in Ireland is privately owned and you are allowed there by concessions granted by various landowners. Please respect this situation and whilst walking there do nothing untoward that might inadvertently damage the delicate goodwill that exists between the vast majority of these landowners and walkers who tread across their lands. In particular, in Beara certain waymarked walks have been opened up that depend upon concessionary rights granted by sheep farmers and others. Here, restricted access is allowed by these landowners on the strict understanding that walkers will not be accompanied by dogs, not even those on leads, whilst crossing over their land along designated ways. Therefore, when walking in this peninsula please check with the local tourist office as to where this restriction on dogs applies.

A few observations now about the crucial matter of safety, for I have long maintained that the bottom line of any walk, including short ones, is safety, with enjoyment positioned just above this! Therefore, always set out well prepared with the right clothes, plenty of food and drink, and a clear but flexible plan in your head as to where you are going that day. In most instances, the two most important aspects of outdoor clothing are to wear comfortable boots and to have robust waterproofs handy. Fortunately, nowadays there are several excellent makes of these items to choose from, all quite competitively priced. For the record, I prefer to wear Brasher mountain boots and socks and Sprayway outdoor clothing, and I have been protected by these for many years now, remaining comfortable and dry within them, even in the foulest of weathers. I would also recommend the use of walking poles, and again, based on highly favourable experiences, the Brasher ones are my preference.

The other two absolute essentials, particularly when you are crossing open, featureless terrain, are detailed, waterproofed maps of the area and a reliable compass. I also carry a torch, a whistle, a warm, woollen ski hat and thermal mittens at all times, even during the hottest days of summer! Depending on the time of the year and when necessary, consider taking at least factor 12 sun-cream, sun-glasses, protective headgear, insect repellent, isotonic drinks and the like. Without burdening yourselves unnecessarily, for some items can be shared within a party of walkers, stow all of these items that you do not immediately need into a well-balanced, framed rucksack that contains a good-quality waterproof lining. Finally on the important subject of looking after yourselves, always obtain a local weather forecast before you set out and be influenced by this.

My wish is that this collection of 20 short walks and the way these are presented will provide further purpose and inspiration to those who have previously trod these ways, as well as an irresistible incentive for others to do the same. Should these wishes be realised, my endeavours will have been well rewarded. Good luck with whatever achievements this book motivates you to attain, and always return ready for the off again and looking forward to more.

ACKNOWLEDGMENTS

'To know all things is not permitted.'
Horace (65–8 B.C.)

Again, it gives me pleasure to record my gratitude to the many kind people, both sides of the Irish Sea, who have so expertly and generously contributed to this book. To all of the people concerned may I express my warm thanks and sincerely record that without their valuable contributions so agreeably provided this book simply would not have been published.

These people include those who have guided me on my way, those who have provided shelter and sustenance to my wife and I, those who have opened doors that might otherwise have remained closed, those who have helped with travel arrangements, and those who have either contributed important material for the book, copy-edited the text or checked the manuscript and proofs. To each and all of you, many thanks.

My special thanks are due to Christopher Stacey, Michael Desmond, Connie Doyle, John Gerard O'Sullivan, Johnny Walsh, Michael O'Shea, Tony O'Callaghan of South West Walks, Timothy Paul Ó Conchúir and Christopher Browne for either telling me where to place my footsteps or, better still, showing me exactly the routes along which to do just this; to Maura Byrne, Mary and Seamus Wall, Bríd Casey and Rose Rima who have been exceptionally kind and generous within a much larger band of people who have helped greatly with our accommodation needs; and to Stena Line Ltd for whizzing us, on several occasions, across the Irish Sea so fast and in such comfortable surroundings.

Bill Rouse, a great friend and walking companion for many years, has again expertly produced the innovative, computer-generated diagrams that do so much to enhance the presentation of each of the walks, and once more I must applaud his more than perfectionist approach to completing this task.

The manuscript of the book was meticulously audited by Eddie Fidler, another long-standing friend and expert walker, and he too deserves his contribution to be recorded and appreciated by me. Also, Finbarr O'Shea, my copy-editor, has made another meticulous and perceptive contribution to the finished work.

My final debt of gratitude must be to my wife Bridget, whose parents happen to come from Ireland, and to our two daughters Katrina and Helen. These three happy souls not only have accompanied and helped me on many of the walks but also have put up with the subsequent long periods when I inevitably neglected them whilst I was preoccupied with peering at my computer screen as I recorded these joyous walking experiences to share with others of similar inclination.

UNDERSTANDING AND USING THE BOOK

'Understanding is the beginning of approving.'
André Gide

The core of this book is a collection of varied short walks that comprehensively covers the mountainous regions of Ireland stretching from the rounded granite domes of Co Wicklow in the east to the pointed quartzite peaks of Connemara and Co Mayo in the west. In between these locations the walks explore the Nire Valley and the rugged surrounding terrain of the Comeragh and Knockmealdown Mountains, range across the magnificent coastal scenery of the south-western peninsulas of Beara, Iveragh and Dingle, and roam around the Killarney National Park.

In addition to providing terrain that is ideal for short walking, each of the areas visited contains numerous places of interest associated with the great outdoors, and walks have been selected that may conveniently be combined with visiting one or more of these attractions, some of which will have special appeal to children and to family groups.

The walks are presented clearly and concisely with illustrative diagrams and colour photographs to provide an appealing and authoritative compilation of routes, some familiar and others relatively new.

THE CLIFFS AND A SANDY BEACH AT SLEA HEAD, CO KERRY

Detailed route descriptions are provided and features of interest are pointed out along the way as these are first observed, given favourable weather. Brief details are also provided of the associated places of interest that may be either incorporated into the walking route or visited whilst in the vicinity.

IRELAND
The Walking Areas Covered

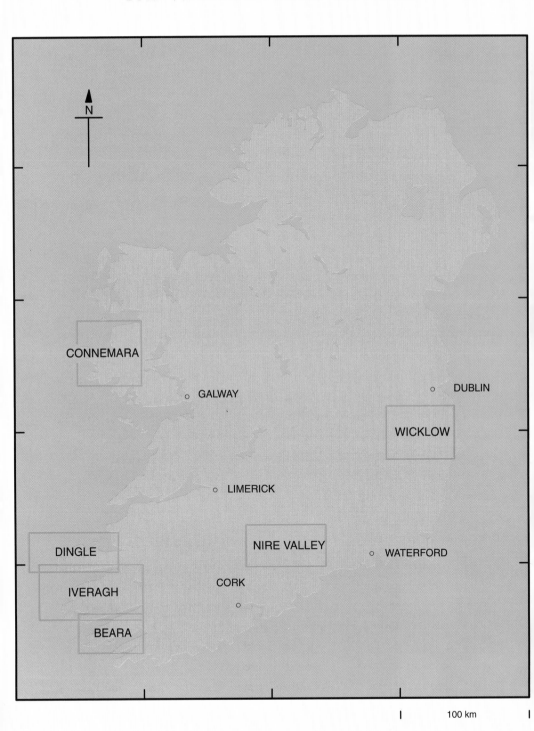

N

CONNEMARA

GALWAY

DUBLIN

WICKLOW

LIMERICK

DINGLE

NIRE VALLEY

WATERFORD

IVERAGH

CORK

BEARA

100 km

Arrangement and Composition

In total, 20 walking routes are included. The distribution of these over six separate areas is shown in the following table.

Walking Area	Number of Walks
Wicklow and the Wicklow Mountains	4
Nire Valley and the Comeragh and Knockmealdown Mountains	3
Beara Peninsula	3
Killarney Lakes and Iveragh Peninsula (Ring of Kerry)	3
Dingle Peninsula	3
Connemara and Mayo	4
Total	**20**

Apart from the wide geographical coverage, the collection of walks also encompasses a broad spectrum of varying degrees of challenge. Within the overall classification of short walks, at one extreme are routes which demand minimum effort, being low-level walks within valleys or around sheltered lakes, and these are graded as easy/straightforward, whilst at the other extreme there are routes which lead up to the summit of a modest hill or mountain and which may necessitate covering some exposed ground, and these are graded as moderate/challenging.

Most of the walks start from a conveniently located car park or lay-by, and details of the size of these and of amenities available there, such as toilets, picnic areas, eating facilities, gift shops and information centres, are provided.

In total the 20 walks cover 140 km (87 miles). The cumulative height climbed is over 6110 m (over 20 000 ft).

Introduction and General Information

The layout of each of the six walking areas starts with an introduction that provides pertinent information to walkers and to more general tourists about the landscapes of that area, its suitability for short walks, places of interest and other details that should be helpful to those going there with the intention of stretching their legs. This is arranged under the subheadings of Landscapes and Opportunities for Short Walks; Places of Interest Associated with Walking and the Great Outdoors; Choice of Walks and Associated Places of Interest; and Walking Guides, Accommodation and Eating Out.

Some people may feel that expert, local walking guides are not needed for short walks. Certainly, short walks, by their very nature, will not venture across remote terrain nor climb to the greatest heights, and in this regard they obviously do not involve the same degree of risk as more demanding, lengthier walks that often cross rough, high-level ground and scale craggy, exposed mountain peaks. Nevertheless, the author consulted and walked with guides or local farmers in all the areas covered in the book and he benefited greatly from this companionship. Routes were suggested, things of interest pointed out, places visited, people met and a comradeship generated that would not have been possible from a 'do it alone' approach. Based on these agreeable experiences it is recommended, particularly if you are going to an area for the first time, that you walk with a local guide on at least one occasion whilst there. Following this, you will be much better informed in deciding whether you wish to continue under formal escort or blaze a trail of your own.

A POWERSCOURT WATERFALL, CO WICKLOW

The author has stayed at most of the accommodation establishments listed and he has personally visited and been shown around the remaining few, each of which has been recommended to him by a reliable source. All these establishments have a special empathy towards walkers and their needs, such as drying wet clothes and providing packed lunches, and without question you will be made very welcome at each of these. All of these establishments are very good indeed, maintaining the highest of standards, and the best are quite superb, often being located in places of exceptional natural beauty where tranquillity abounds. (Given this glowing testimony, perhaps it should be pointed out that not all of the places that the author has stayed at overnight in Ireland have been included in these accommodation registers!)

WALKING ROUTES

The information provided for each walk commences with a concise 'Fact File' which, in easy-to-assimilate, tabular format, provides details of Start/Finish; Grading; Walking Time Allowance; Distance; Total Height Gained; and Highest

Point. Distances and heights are stated first in metric measurements, followed by their imperial equivalents which have been rounded off. The metric heights are taken from the relevant Ordnance Survey Ireland Discovery Series maps and the imperial equivalents have been calculated from these using a conversion factor of 0.3048 m equals 1 ft, rounded off to the nearest 5 ft.

A 'Digest of Walk' follows which provides summary information covering Parking; Overview/Interest; Gradients; Amenities; Maps, Footpaths and Waysigns; and Getting Started. Then there are suggestions for organising the walk and excursion, and this section is followed by the main description of the walk, which includes detailed route-finding directions. The suitability of the walk and visits to associated places of interest is then discussed, and, finally, brief details of these places of interest are provided.

GRADING OF WALKS

A number of factors will affect how difficult or otherwise a particular walk is to each walking party. These include the time of year, the weather and ground conditions on the day, and the walkers' age and physical condition, walking ability and experience, knowledge of the area, and map-reading and compass-reading capabilities.

Nevertheless, and bearing in mind that all the walks included in the book are considered to be

Λ LOOKING NORTHWARDS TOWARDS THE GAP OF DUNLOE, CO KERRY

short ones, each walk has been graded as either 'easy/straightforward' or 'moderate/challenging' to provide some sort of benchmark of 'what to expect' that will be helpful to walkers, particularly those who are not familiar with the countryside through which the walk passes. This classification is considered to be relative rather than absolute and when a walk is considered to be on the borderline between the two categories, this is indicated. The criteria on which the grading is based are disclosed below.

- Easy/straightforward (colour-coded BLUE). These walks are for the most part along fairly level ground, with no sustained, severe uphill gradients. Where modest climbs are involved these are well spaced out, with ample recovery distances in between. There is no potentially dangerous exposure or

difficult terrain of any consequence, and the route avoids waterlogged ground and boggy areas wherever possible. Route finding presents few problems on these walks, paths are followed for much of the way, and there are adequate signs or marker cairns where needed. These walks are frequently suitable for family groups, and often have plenty of general interest in addition to the surrounding views and countryside.

↗ THE GLENNAHOO RIVER AND VALLEY SWEEPING PAST THE PEAK OF BEENBO, CO KERRY

- Moderate/challenging (colour-coded RED). These walks are suitable for all reasonably fit participants who wish to follow a route that could take a good half-day or so to complete. However, they do contain a combination of features that makes them significantly more exacting than the previous category. These features could be some sustained or energetic climbing, more exposure, waterlogged or boggy ground and a longer, more complicated route, parts of which are less clearly signed. On occasions these walks will cross rough, open ground where there are no obvious paths and this will provide a taste of more adventurous walking. This category of walks is less suitable for younger children but could appeal greatly to older, stronger youngsters who are accompanied by experienced adults.

WALKING TIME ALLOWANCE

Estimates of walking time have been provided for each route, but they do not include allowances for prolonged stops such as coffee breaks, lunch or spending time on a beach. The estimates are generous and have been calculated by allowing 1 hour to walk each 3 km (almost 2 miles) and a further half an hour for each 250 m (820 ft) climbed, with a final adjustment of up to plus or minus half an hour per walk depending upon additional factors such as relative ease or difficulty of route finding, state of the path, roughness of the terrain and so on. With experience, these basic estimates may be adjusted to suit your own preferred walking speed.

DIAGRAMS

A diagram is provided for each route and this gives both a plan and a cross-sectional relief of the walk. These diagrams have been computer generated and are based upon grid reference points downloaded from Ordnance Survey Ireland maps, the Discovery Series 1:50 000 — 2 cm to 1 km ($1\frac{1}{4}$ inches to 1 mile). The relief cross-section has been constructed from the contour lines provided on the Ordnance Survey maps and the profile, commencing from the start of the walk, accurately follows the exact line of the route.

Camera symbols in the diagrams locate the position and direction of take of each photograph that illustrates the walk. These have been allocated a number identical to that appearing beneath each photograph as part of its caption within the book. The first part of the number indicates the route, whilst the second part refers to the sequence of the photographs within each route. Photographs taken from the route are indicated by the camera symbol pointing either along or away from the line of the walk, whereas photographs taken of the route from other vantage points are identified by the camera symbol pointing inwards towards the line of the walk.

PHOTOGRAPHS

On average two colour photographs illustrate each walk and each of the walking areas is introduced by a large double-page view. The illustrative photographs of the walk are keyed in to the route to provide additional aids to route finding. The photographs have been taken throughout the seasons and a balance has been struck between those that show landscapes and other features of interest only and those that contain a human element in the shape of walkers.

The photographs have been taken with a Canon EOS 650 camera using 50 mm fixed focus and 35–135 zoom lens. In each case the exposures have been shot through polarising filters. Fujichrome, Sensia 100 colour slide film has been used exclusively. (The author finds this particular combination of camera and film ideal for outdoor landscape photography and has been using it for several years now.)

THE CLIFFS OF MOHER CAPPED BY O'BRIEN'S TOWER, CO CLARE

ABBREVIATIONS

Abbreviations are used sparingly in the book, and then only to avoid constant repetition of easily identified words. These are listed below, and they include familiar direction signals, compass bearings and measurements.

Abbreviations		Abbreviations	
L	left	W	west
R	right	WNW	west-north-west
N	north	NW	north-west
NNE	north-north-east	NNW	north-north-west
NE	north-east	cm	centimetre(s)
ENE	east-north-east	ft	foot/feet
E	east	hrs	hours
ESE	east-south-east	km	kilometre(s)
SE	south-east	m	metre(s)
SSE	south-south-east	mm	millimetre(s)
S	south	sq	square
SSW	south-south-west	MR	map reference
SW	south-west	OS	Ordnance Survey
WSW	west-south-west	YH	youth hostel

MAPS AND COMPASS

No guidebook is an adequate substitute for maps and a compass but rather should be used in conjunction with these aids. Use the Ordnance Survey Ireland Discovery Series maps, scale 1:50 000, previously referred to and a reliable compass at all times when you are walking across open countryside and particularly when there is confusing mist and low cloud swirling about. There are also some larger scale 1:25 000 maps available, such as that covering the Killarney National Park, and substitute these wherever this is possible.

The full complement of OS Discovery Series maps needed to cover all of the 20 walks described in this book are Numbers 30, 31, 37, 38, 44, 56, 70, 74, 75, 78, 83 and 84, twelve maps in all. These maps are excellent but not infallible! On the rare occasions where there are differences between the route descriptions provided in the book and the position of the paths shown, or not shown, as the case may be, on the OS maps, rely on the route descriptions.

Additionally, the Ordnance Survey produces four Holiday maps, with the smaller scale of 1:250 000, and these also depict the relief of the countryside, albeit in broader bands. These maps are ideal for completing the road journeys between the various areas covered by the book, and for this purpose you will need Numbers 2, 3 and 4.

All compass bearings are given to the nearest $22\frac{1}{2}$-degree point, for example N, NNE, NE etc. This is considered to be sufficiently accurate over the relatively small distances travelled between the taking of successive readings. When crossing featureless terrain, particularly in bad weather, do take frequent compass bearings when necessary so that you always know where you are and the direction in which to proceed.

Human Constructions

Individual features of the countryside, particularly human-constructed ones, are constantly changing: fences appear where there were none before, gates replace stiles and vice versa, additional waymarker signs are positioned, some indicators like cairns may collapse and so on. Therefore, in the passage of time you will almost inevitably come across isolated differences between the route descriptions that appear in this guidebook and what you encounter on location! When you do, presume that these have occurred since the book went to press and proceed with confidence to the next certain feature described.

Spelling of Place-names

Often there is more than one version of the spelling of a place-name and occasionally there are multiple choices. In such instances the spelling that appears on the OS Discovery Series maps is used, unless otherwise indicated.

Places of Interest

Finally, at the end of each of the routes, brief details are provided of the associated places of interest in the area that might be conveniently included in the walk. These include visiting stately homes, walking around natural gardens, crossing the waves to nearby islands, spending time looking around aquariums, absorbing information on display at interpretative centres, looking around major visitor attractions and just relaxing on a fine, sandy beach.

Contact information for each of these places of interest is given, and should you intend taking a large party to any of these visitor attractions, it will obviously be in your interest to make prior contact with those in charge and to obtain any concessionary admission charges that are on offer for such groups.

V OVERLEAF: THE INFANT RIVER LIFFEY GURGLING THROUGH RURAL SCENERY IN WICKLOW

WICKLOW
WALKS

WICKLOW WALKS

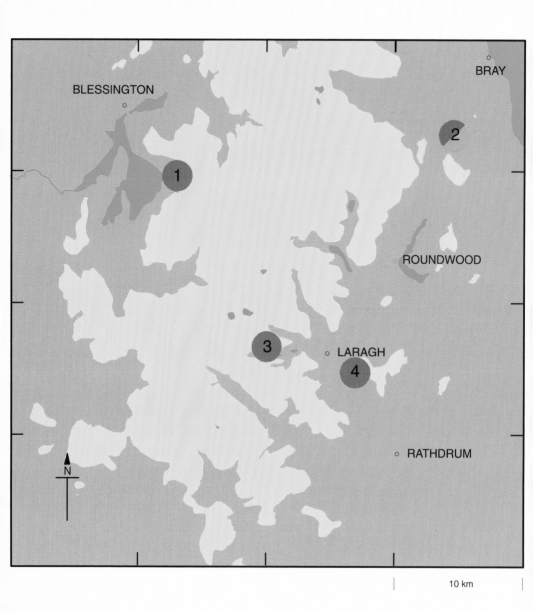

BRAY

BLESSINGTON

2

1

ROUNDWOOD

3

LARAGH

4

N

RATHDRUM

10 km

Wicklow and the Wicklow Mountains

Landscapes and Opportunities for Short Walks

Much of Co Wicklow is dominated by the vast landscapes of the Wicklow Mountains. These gigantic mounds of granite rise just a few miles to the S of the sprawling suburbs of Dublin city, from where they extend, roughly south-westwards, for some 35 km (over 20 miles). In this process they progressively gain height to form the majestic summit area of Lugnaquillia Mountain, which, at 925 m (3035 ft), is one of only 12 peaks to soar above 3000 ft in the whole of Ireland. The greater part of this high, undulating terrain is covered with difficult, boggy ground, and this, together with access problems, renders it unsuitable territory for short walks.

Not so are the fringes of these mountains! Here, particularly along the eastern and western flanks of this upthrust ground, there is a variety of terrain that is ideal for short walks. The walking possibilities here will appeal to most people who love to stretch their legs, be this an energetic climb to the top of an exposed hill or mountain, or just a leisurely stroll beside the tranquil waters of a lovely, secluded lake.

The eastern slopes of the Wicklow Mountains are punctuated by a series of deep, glaciated valleys including Glenmacnass, Glendasan, Glendalough and Glenmalure. Exploring these forested slopes, discovering spectacular corrie loughs, observing gurgling mountain streams and watching waterfalls cascading down precipitously steep rock faces, provides a multitude of fascinating, short walking routes of varying grades of difficulty amongst magnificent mountain scenery. The land sweeping down on the western side of the Wicklow Mountains is more gentle, and here wide, spacious valleys liberally covered with forests and farmlands provide alternative walking areas that again support a variety of short explorations on foot to suit most tastes. These hilly landscapes surround the eastern reaches of the vast Pollaphuca Reservoir complex near Blessington, and with a scenic drive and ample parking areas provided along the attractive shores of these waters, further possibilities for short, leisurely strolls and picnicking have more recently been opened up hereabouts.

Places of Interest Associated with Walking and the Great Outdoors

Wicklow deserves being described as 'The Garden of Ireland'. This colourful land of wafting blooms includes both world-famous formal gardens laid out on the grand scale such as Powerscourt and the most delightful natural habitats like the one nurtured with tender, loving care at Mount Usher. There are also the lovely, shaded glades and woodlands of Avondale parklands to cushion your footsteps as you leisurely wander through this deciduous wonderland.

There are a number of other great houses and gardens in Wicklow, including Kilruddery, with its seventeenth-century layout, Russborough, with its famed paintings by Goya, Rubens and Velázquez, and Dargle Glen, which also houses important works of art. There is a superbly appointed interpretative centre located at Glendalough which is dedicated to explaining monastic settlements, in particular the nearby holy site founded by St Kevin in the sixth century.

The National Adventure Centre is located at Tiglin, near Ashford, and there is a Lakes Pursuit Centre near Blessington. Other outdoor activities include rock climbing, cycling, pony trekking, golf, angling, sailing and bathing from both sandy and shingle beaches.

Choice of Walks and Associated Places of Interest

An exploration of Glendalough just had to be included in the book, and this is provided by Walk 3 as it leads excitingly up by Pollanass Waterfall to The Spink. Standing on the top of the isolated peak of Great Sugar Loaf also proved to be irresistible, and this is combined with a visit to nearby Powerscourt House, Gardens and Waterfall in Walk 2. Walk 4, a climb to the summit of Trooperstown Hill, is another outing on the eastern side of the Wicklow Mountains. By contrast Walk 1, an energetic circuit of Black Hill above Pollaphuca Reservoir, attempts to redress the balance somewhat, by leading you around part of the western side of the mountains.

Walking Guides, Accommodation and Eating Out

WALKING GUIDES

Apart from joyously participating in several Wicklow Walking Festivals, the only guide I have used to explore this region, this now on numerous occasions, is

Christopher Stacey. Christopher is a forester by trade and an enthusiastic member of the local Glen of Imaal Mountain Rescue Team. He has also built up a highly successful guiding business under the banner of 'Footfalls'. This team are very professional, and in their expert care you will walk in comparative safety and have pointed out to you much of the flora and fauna that you might otherwise pass by unnoticed. You will also have great fun, both as you walk along and later on as you attempt to recuperate each evening in traditional ways that are best known only to the Irish!

CONTACT DETAILS

Christopher Stacey
'Footfalls'
Trooperstown
Roundwood
Co Wicklow
Tel/Fax: 0404 45152
Email: cstacey@iol.ie
Web site: http://ireland.iol.ie/~cstacey

ACCOMMODATION

In and around the village of Laragh is a good, central location for exploring the hill-walking delights of Wicklow and the Wicklow Mountains. Other attractive places for doing this are from the Blessington, Valleymount, Hollywood and Donard area to the W of the mountains, in and near to Roundwood in the E, and at Rathdrum and along the Vale of Avoca to the SE.

Listed below are some of our favourite places to stay. These all have a special empathy towards the needs of walkers and I can guarantee that Maura Byrne at 'Escombe', Liz Smith and Des Kennedy at 'Tudor Lodge' and Teresa Kavanagh at 'Derrybawn Mountain Lodge' will extend particularly warm welcomes to you, whether you are togged in dripping wet walking gear or otherwise.

ACCOMMODATION REGISTER

Hotel/Guest House	Rooms en suite		Rooms other		Open
Maura Byrne Escombe Country House Lockstown Valleymount Glendalough Road Co Wicklow Tel: 045 867157 Fax: 045 867450	F D T S	4 1 1 0	F D T S	0 0 0 0	All year

Hotel/Guest House	Rooms en suite		Rooms other		Open
Liz Smith and Des Kennedy Tudor Lodge Laragh Glendalough Co Wicklow Tel/Fax: 0404 45554	F D T S	3 4 1 2	F D T S	0 0 0 0	All year
Teresa Kavanagh Derrybawn Mountain Lodge Derrybawn Laragh Glendalough Co Wicklow Tel: 0404 45644 Fax: 0404 45645	F D T S	8 0 0 0	F D T S	0 0 0 0	All year
Pat and Ann Dowling Glenmalure Lodge Glenmalure Rathdrum Co Wicklow Tel/Fax: 0404 46188	F D T S	0 2 7 0	F D T S	2 0 0 1	All year

Rooms: F = Family; D = Double; T = Twin; S = Single

EATING OUT

There are a variety of good restaurants, pubs and eating places in and around Laragh that should satisfy most tastes and come within your purse range. Those we have tried and liked include the Wicklow Heather Restaurant (Tel: 0404 45157), which boasts an extensive menu, and Lynham's Inn (Tel: 0404 45345), where you can eat good, wholesome bar food with not too far to go for a drink with which to wash it down.

The traditional Glenmalure Lodge near Rathdrum (Tel: 0404 46188) will serve walkers with the likes of tender steak and crispy chips after they have descended, famished, into this remote and sublime valley, whilst on t'other side of the mountains, delicious, value-for-money bar meals are also available at the elegant Tulfarris House Hotel and Country Club (Tel: 045 864574) overlooking Pollaphuca Reservoir.

BLACK HILL
(AND POLLAPHUCA RESERVOIR)

fact/ile

START/FINISH
Car park adjacent to mountain road —
MR 044108

GRADING
Moderate/challenging (colour-coded
RED)

WALKING TIME ALLOWANCE
3.5 hours

DISTANCE
7.7 km (4.8 miles)

TOTAL HEIGHT GAINED
330 m (1085 ft)

HIGHEST POINT
Black Hill — 602 m (1975 ft)

digest o/walk

PARKING
Small, isolated car park holds about 10 cars.

OVERVIEW/INTEREST
- Start is amongst vast, open landscapes that form wild and rugged mountain countryside.
- Absorbing, panoramic, long-distance views for most of the way, given clear weather.
- Bird's-eye perspectives of indented Pollaphuca Reservoir.
- Visit to the site of an aeroplane crash.
- Route passes by a disused limekiln located in farmed pastures.

BLACK HILL
(AND POLLAPHUCA RESERVOIR)

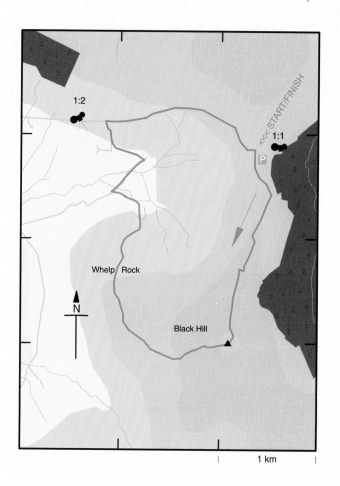

1 km

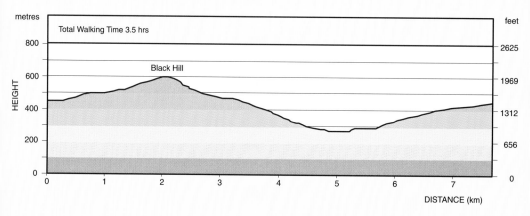

GRADIENTS

A gradual climb to the top of Black Hill with a similar descent. Some steeper and rougher sections near the top.

AMENITIES

None.

MAPS, FOOTPATHS AND WAYSIGNS

OS DISCOVERY SERIES 1:50 000 — NUMBER 56 (WICKLOW, DUBLIN AND KILDARE)

The route varies, with extremes ranging from following a combination of wide, obvious tracks, paths and minor roads to walking across areas of uncharted moorlands. Some exposed, boggy ground has to be crossed, but unless there has been recent heavy rain this does not present formidable difficulties. The most challenging section is on the higher ground around the summit of Black Hill.

Waysigns are non-existent and there is only one summit cairn to confirm where you are!

GETTING STARTED

The starting-point of the walk lies some 3 km (nearly 2 miles) to the E of Pollaphuca Reservoir near the top of the gap separating Black Hill to the S from Sorrel Hill to the N. The usual approach is along the minor road from Lackan, by turning off the scenic drive around Pollaphuca Reservoir. However, the start can be reached by motoring S along the minor roads leading up from the R759.

Depart from the car park along the broad track that winds S directly towards the summit of Black Hill.

ORGANISATION OF WALK AND ASSOCIATED EXCURSION

This half-day, energetic walk to the summit of Black Hill may be conveniently combined with leisurely motoring around the attractive Pollaphuca Reservoir. You may do this keeping fairly close to the water's edge travelling along the scenic drive and *en route* perhaps stopping at the Blessington Leisure Centre (see 'Places of Interest' below). From here you may take a relaxing cruise on the MV *Blessington* waterbus. If possible, complete the walk in the morning, thereby leaving the rest of the day to explore the diverse attractions surrounding the massive reservoir complex.

DESCRIPTION OF WALK

The placid waters of the irregular-shaped Pollaphuca Reservoir fill the valley down below to the W as you set off from the parking area, whilst in the opposite direction, towards SE, a rounded, massive mountain spur progressively gains height to culminate in the vastness of Mullaghcleevaun. This mountain at 849 m (2785 ft) is the highest point in view, assuming the weather is favourable, as you set off. Your principal objective for the day, the summit of Black Hill, lies just to the W of due S in the form of a vast, rounded dome.

The way there along a wide path, which is surfaced with compacted, sandy shale and small stones, snakes across the heather-covered hillsides, gaining height up a gentle gradient. As you progress, look to your L above the intervening conifers to spot the telecommunications masts located on the vast summit of Kippure, far away to the NE. More secrets of the surrounding rugged mountain scenery will be progressively revealed as you climb higher.

Further on, be careful to avoid being led astray by a side track leading off on the L. Beyond this your track skirts by a tiny bog pool to your R, and, having ignored a turning off to the R, continue to head uphill allowing the track to lead you into an area of granite outcrops and small boulders, where it abruptly terminates! From here continue SSW, still climbing, as you cross more demanding terrain in the form of heather moorlands criss-crossed with peat channels and quite often areas of waterlogged ground. Fortunately, only a short distance now separates you from the summit of Black Hill.

1:1 INQUISITIVE OCCUPANTS OF THE GENTLE APPROACH SLOPES OF BLACK HILL

A walk along a shallow, eroded ditch will lead you to the top of the mountain. This is a flattish, almost featureless, vast, rounded summit area punctuated by a tiny cairn of stones. In the wet season this mound rises out of a surrounding moat filled by a black, oozy pool of peat. You are now standing at a height of 602 m (1975 ft), and in clear weather the all-round panoramas from this lofty viewing platform are quite superb. Most of the highlights have already been positioned, but there are revealing new vistas from here including far away to the SSE the distinctive straight edge of the reservoir straddling Fair Mountain and Camaderry which is located high above the Wicklow Gap. Much nearer, the rounded hillsides of Moanbane rise invitingly to the SSW.

From the certain landmark of the cairn, head downhill, walking due W. The initial part of the descent is quite exacting across expansive, uncharted slopes covered with tufted grasses and heather. Watch out for the occasional bog hole in this vicinity! The downwards slopes steepen slightly as you continue to track W, now following the crest of a broad band of protruding ground that has developed above the immediately surrounding slopes. Further down, the gradient begins to level off as your descent tracks through an area where peat is harvested. (The locals tell me this is the best peat in all of Ireland, but you may know differently!)

Further on, you will spot what looks like a tall marker post, and when you do, trim your line of descent to walk directly towards this landmark, where you will connect with a wide track. (Note: The position and number of tracks/paths shown on the OS map in this vicinity are not strictly accurate and so be careful hereabouts!) When you get there you will discover that the post is in fact a fine slab of granite and that this marks the crash site of a Hamden bomber. The plane came down on 18 April 1941 killing Pilot Officer J K Hill and Sergeants J T Hill, J T Lamb and S Wright. The poignant memorial was placed there fifty years later, in April 1991.

Turn R along the wide, secure track and follow it as it loops around towards NW surrendering further height. The continuation descent then curves further to the R changing your direction of progress to N, and as it does so the most revealing views westwards of the entire sweep of Pollaphuca Reservoir come into sight. From here, you will see that these trapped waters are twice almost cut in two by the twin peninsulas of Valleymount and Boystown. Two attractive arched bridges span the intervening narrow straits of water and these provide convenient road access right around the reservoir.

A grassy surface develops along the descent track as orderly, farmed pastures come into view below. Rising above these on the far side of the valley to the NNE are the rounded features of Sorrel Hill. Continue walking downhill towards the cluster of farmsteads below which are located towards the head of a wide, fertile valley. A small group of hardy trees shelter the upper reaches of this valley, a quite unusual feature in this rugged terrain which is generally above the tree line. The green track leads down to a metal gate that you need to pass through, heeding the sign to close it afterwards!

1:2 THE DESCENT CROSSES THE VAST BOWL AT KILBEG TO THE WEST OF THE SUMMIT OF BLACK HILL

From here, continue downhill to pass by, on your R, a group of residences which accommodate barking dogs! The descent then connects with a better-defined track, which you bear R along. This will lead you further down to reach a second gate, which you should also ensure is closed after use. Now turn L, in the opposite direction to a cattle grid, to walk NW further downhill along a twisting, banked lane. This will bring you to a T-junction, where you turn R along a side lane that winds uphill to the NE passing between gorse thickets. A small gushing stream is then bridged and beyond this the continuation route rises further to pass by more dwellings on your R.

After bridging a second small stream, proceed through an iron gate on your L. This barrier is held in position with a variety of strings and ropes which you will need to refasten after use. From here, a green road snakes uphill on a diagonal course to the NW to lead you past an interesting, disused limekiln. This is V-shaped and built from granite. Bear R uphill beyond this feature to locate and pass through a gateway in the far hedge of the field. After this, turn L to use another metal gate that provides access to farm buildings. A third iron gate allows you to reach a lane ahead, which you turn R along to continue your way northwards climbing a moderate gradient.

Past a redundant gateway, the farm access lane winds up to a minor road a short distance above. Turn R here and a more comfortable slope will lead you eastwards back to the parking area that is now just over 1½ km (1 mile) away.

SUITABILITY OF WALK AND ASSOCIATED PLACES OF INTEREST FOR FAMILIES

The complete walk is fine for sturdy teenagers but is probably too tough for younger children. Families with small ones might venture some way towards Black Hill, perhaps as far as where the secure track ends, and then retrace their steps back to the parking area.

The scenic drive around Pollaphuca Reservoir with its attractively located parking spots and screened picnic areas should appeal to all, and most children should find something to please and interest them at Blessington Leisure Centre.

PLACES OF INTEREST

BLESSINGTON LEISURE CENTRE

This centre, located at MR 980134 and marked as Blessington Lakes Pursuits Centre on the OS map, provides land and water facilities for visitors to enjoy the magnificent surrounding lakes, forests and mountains at their best. Activities offered at the centre include archery, orienteering, abseiling and rock climbing, pony trekking, quad biking, windsurfing, sailing, kayaking and Canadian canoeing. There are luxury holiday homes located on-site, and a restaurant and coffee shop overlooks the private marina. For further information contact:

Blessington Land and Water Sports
Burgage
Blessington
Co Wicklow
Tel: 045 865800
Fax: 045 865024

MV BLESSINGTON

The MV *Blessington* is an all-weather, 78-seater waterbus that provides one-hour cruises around the lake departing from Blessington Leisure Centre. These cruises provide unique views of the surrounding, alluring countryside, and a live commentary of the history and folklore of the area is given.

GREAT SUGAR LOAF
(AND POWERSCOURT HOUSE, GARDENS AND WATERFALL)

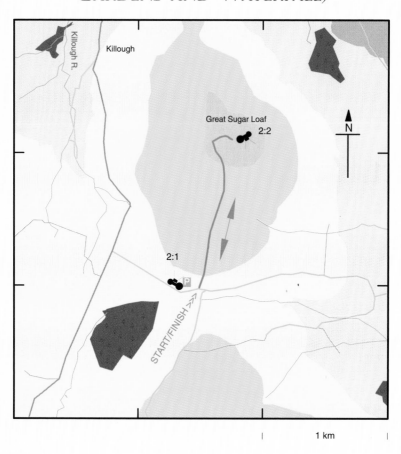

Killough R.

Killough

Great Sugar Loaf

2:2

N

2:1

P

START/FINISH

1 km

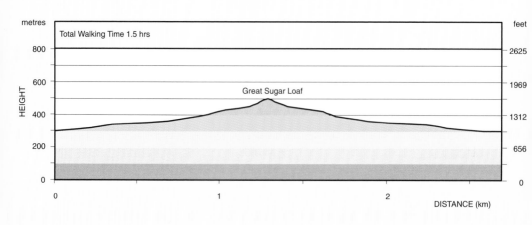

Total Walking Time 1.5 hrs

Great Sugar Loaf

metres — feet

800 — 2625

600 — 1969

400 — 1312

200 — 656

0 — 0

HEIGHT

0   1   2

DISTANCE (km)

GREAT SUGAR LOAF (AND POWERSCOURT HOUSE, GARDENS AND WATERFALL)

ORGANISATION OF WALK AND ASSOCIATED

fact/ile

START/FINISH
Car park off R755 road —
MR 234121

GRADING
Easy/straightforward to moderate/ challenging, depending upon fitness (colour-coded BLUE/RED)

WALKING TIME ALLOWANCE
1.5 hours

DISTANCE
2.7 km (1.7 miles)

TOTAL HEIGHT GAINED
210 m (690 ft)

HIGHEST POINT
Great Sugar Loaf — 501 m (1645 ft)

digest/o/walk

PARKING
Massive parking area but narrow entrance between boulders that prevents wide vehicles such as mobile homes from entering.

OVERVIEW/INTEREST

- Energetic climb to the top of an isolated mountain peak.
- The craggy summit area makes a superb viewing platform given favourable weather.
- Excellent views of the nearby coastal strip and inland towards the Wicklow Mountains.
- Convenient access makes this a short, sharp up-and-down suitable for evening exercise.
- A rocky gully leads to the summit affording opportunities for easy, unexposed scrambling.

GRADIENTS

Following a gentle, easy start, the approach incline progressively steepens, as the ground becomes rougher. The final climb is up a steep, rocky chute where handholds may be required to maintain your balance. The return descent is the reverse of this.

AMENITIES

None, apart from the opportunity to picnic at or near to the large, grassy parking area. (Extensive amenities at nearby Powerscourt House.)

MAPS, FOOTPATHS AND WAYSIGNS

OS DISCOVERY SERIES 1:50 000 — NUMBER 56 (WICKLOW, DUBLIN AND KILDARE)

An obvious, well-trod, wide, grassy path snakes across the short distance to the foot of Great Sugar Loaf. From here, a rougher, stony track winds up the steepening slopes to then zigzag up a narrow gully lined with fixed rock outcrops and a mixture of loose scree, stones and boulders. The ground underfoot is well drained all the way, although some erosion has to be contended with, due to heavy usage!

There are no signs *en route* but none are needed.

GETTING STARTED

The starting-point is along a minor road to the E of the R755 road between the village of Roundwood to the S and Kilmacanoge to the N on the main, coastal N11 highway. The R759 road via Sally Gap provides links from the W.

From the top edge of the parking area, climb over a stile positioned adjacent to a metal gate, walk northwards up the obvious, wide path and you are on your way.

Excursion

Great Sugar Loaf Mountain, Powerscourt House and Gardens and the nearby Powerscourt Waterfall are all situated in a compact triangle just to the S–SW of Bray and Enniskerry. A visit to these popular attractions and an energetic walk to the top of this mountain make a splendid day out in fine weather, combining absorbing sightseeing with healthy exercise. Whenever possible, get to Powerscourt Estate early in the morning before the crowds have arrived; that way you can walk at your leisure around the magnificent gardens and have a good look at the house when you have these pretty much to yourselves. Afterwards, motor the short distance to the impressive Powerscourt Waterfalls, perhaps having a picnic lunch there before you wander around this splendid site. Save the ascent of Great Sugar Loaf until the late afternoon or early evening when most other visitors will be coming down as you make your way up, thereby once again having a popular place all to yourselves, on this occasion the summit of a famous mountain. Given a good sunset, this is one of the very best times to be up there anyway, and in these conditions the quite superb panoramic views from the top will reward your efforts for climbing up with generous interest.

Description of Walk

The elevated parking area provides fine all-round views right from the very start of the walk. To the NNE your objective, the pointed summit of Great Sugar Loaf shaped like some giant, whitish-grey pyramid, rises majestically above the surrounding land. Your approach path snakes directly to its base. To the W the symmetrically rounded peaks of Tonduff (both North and South), War Hill, Djouce Mountain and White Hill provide the far-away, undulating horizon, whilst in other directions nearer to, pleasant, rolling pastures obscure, for the time being, any more distant views. A short distance further on, as you climb higher, glimpses of the sea and coastline may be observed over to your R.

The obvious approach way rises gently up a modest gradient as you tread along a wide path surfaced with a mixture of grass, stones and compacted gravel. Further on, ignore a grassy cart track leading off to the L. Then the rate of climb progressively increases and this more challenging slope leads you to an inclined grassy area which is less steep and which affords some temporary respite where you can pause in order to get your breath back! This is also a good spot to turn around to take in the splendid views, weather permitting, to your rear.

Continue climbing as the gradient steepens once again. Follow the well-defined way as it contorts around to the L of the rocky summit cone, gaining

⋀ **2:1** The summit of Great Sugar Loaf

further height quite rapidly as it does so. The approach route then reaches a stony, fairly level platform. Before you tackle the final, rocky section above to the E, turn about to take in the splendid panoramas down below to the SW. Given clear weather you will be able to identify the irregular shape of Vartry Reservoir near to the village of Roundwood, these extensive waters cupped between rolling, green landscapes. Towering above this placid scene and forming the far-distant horizon are the high peaks rising to the SW of the Wicklow Gap. These culminate in mighty Lugnaquillia, which, at over 3000 ft, is the highest mountain in Co Wicklow.

Now veer to the R to climb the final, steepest section of the route. This is eastwards up a rocky slope of loose, shattered debris where you should exercise care not to dislodge stones. At the same time be mindful that walkers above you might cause you to exercise some deft, avoiding action yourself to get out of the way of anything which they may have inadvertently disturbed and which is now falling rapidly towards you! The steep way up funnels into a rocky cleft leading to the top of the mountain, but the scramble up this is never exposed and there are countless choices of where to place each secure footstep and also the occasional steadying handhold.

Suddenly you will emerge on to the craggy summit area, which is surprisingly spacious. However, you will almost certainly have to share this with others, who range from serious walkers to family groups who have just popped up there as part of the day out! Given clear weather, the panoramic views from this lofty spot, standing at a height of 501 m (1645 ft), are quite special. Most of those to the W and S should be familiar to you by now as these have already been pointed out on the way up. In addition to these riveting landscapes, splendid new vistas now open up of the flattish coastal strip contained in the semi-circle from N to S through E. You literally have a bird's-eye view of this, with the conurbations of Bray and Greystones spread-eagled below you to the NE and E respectively.

When you have feasted sufficiently on these many-splendoured sights, simply turn tail and head down, retracing your outward steps back to the parking area.

SUITABILITY OF WALK AND ASSOCIATED PLACES OF INTEREST FOR FAMILIES

The entire day out, as described, ought to go down well with older children who should delight in visiting the various Powerscourt attractions and also thrill from the excitement of climbing and standing on top of Great Sugar Loaf. However, be cautious of taking them up there in windy conditions or when the mountaintop is veiled in clinging mist.

This adventurous climb is definitely out of bounds for tiny tots, although the author has seen families with very young children up there when the weather was fine and benign. However, the sensible advice is save this ascent until they are older, and whilst they are still toddlers allow them to revel in all that Powerscourt has to offer, with perhaps allowing them to paddle under your watchful supervision in a safe place by the banks of the Dargle River some distance below the falls.

PLACES OF INTEREST

POWERSCOURT HOUSE AND GARDENS

This is a major tourist attraction drawing thousands upon thousands of visitors each year. The estate is a pleasing mixture of formal gardens and relaxing woodland glades. In particular, the superb view from the rear of the house down across Triton Lake below with its powerful, ornamental fountain and taking in the distant, perfect shape of Great Sugar Loaf Mountain can have few serious rivals for this sort of scenery, anywhere!

In summary, there are nearly 50 acres of gardens for you to explore, including Japanese and Italian gardens, tree trails and a pet's cemetery. In addition there is a terrace restaurant where delicious refreshments are served, a house exhibition, speciality gift shops, a garden centre, picnic areas and a children's play area.

△ **2:2** LOOKING SOUTH-EAST TOWARDS THE COAST FROM THE SUMMIT OF GREAT SUGAR LOAF

The Powerscourt Estate is situated 12 miles S of Dublin city centre, just off the N11 Dublin to Wexford road beside the village of Enniskerry. The attraction may be reached by the number 44 bus from Hawkins Street, Dublin, or the number 85 bus from the Dart Railway Station at Bray.

For further information contact:

Powerscourt Estate
Enniskerry
Co Wicklow
Tel: 01 204 6000
Web site: http://www.powerscourt.ie

POWERSCOURT WATERFALL

Powerscourt Waterfall is located at MR 197122 about 5 km (3 miles) from Powerscourt House and Gardens. This spectacular cascade, gushing down over smoothed rocky cliffs of some 121 m (395 ft), is the highest waterfall in Ireland. The impressive falls are located in magnificent countryside and are surrounded by woodlands and specimen trees through which sika deer roam. Nature trails abound through the adjacent parkland and an informative guide describes these in some detail. Delightful picnic spots are located beneath shady trees and there are refreshment and toilet facilities. Altogether, this is a spot not to be missed and definitely one to savour.

GLENDALOUGH, POLLANASS WATERFALL AND THE SPINK

fact file

START/FINISH

Glendalough Visitor Centre car park — MR 127968

GRADING

Moderate/challenging (colour-coded RED)

WALKING TIME ALLOWANCE

3.5 hours

DISTANCE

8.3 km (5.2 miles)

TOTAL HEIGHT GAINED

360 m (1180 ft)

HIGHEST POINT

The Spink Ridge — 420 m (1380 ft)

digest of walk

PARKING

Spacious, well laid-out, thoughtfully screened parking area. (Very popular place with visitors and consequently fills up quickly in the summer months and on bank holidays.)

OVERVIEW/INTEREST

- A walk of great variety taking in tranquil Glendalough and the magnificence of The Spink rock.
- An opportunity to explore the world-famous monastic site founded by St Kevin.

GLENDALOUGH, POLLANASS WATERFALL AND THE SPINK

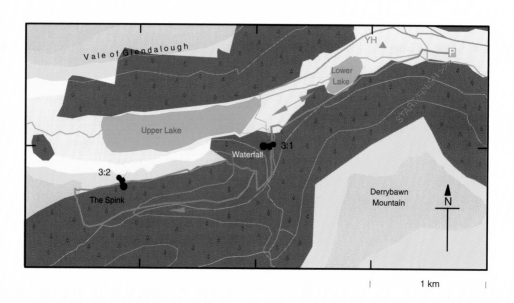

1 km

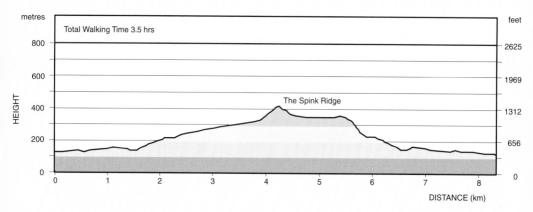

Total Walking Time 3.5 hrs

The Spink Ridge

- The route passes by the spectacular Pollanass Waterfall cascading down a rocky ravine.
- Delightful sections through oak woodlands and pine forests.
- The magnificent landscapes surrounding two contrasting lakes are passed by.
- An abundance of wildlife including sika deer and peregrine falcons.
- Information office and visitor centre providing guided tours of the site.

GRADIENTS

After an initial section virtually on the flat, there is an energetic climb up flights of steps leading beside Pollanass Waterfall. Further on, there is another steep slope through a break in the forest to reach the open ground of The Spink. Following a high-level traverse along the ridge there is a very steep and often quite slippery descent through the forest to arrive back on the lower slopes near to the waterfall.

AMENITIES

Toilet facilities are located at the rear of the visitor centre and there are shaded picnic areas adjacent to the car park. The spacious Glendalough Hotel, situated nearby, serves a variety of delicious refreshments.

MAPS, FOOTPATHS AND WAYSIGNS

OS DISCOVERY SERIES 1:50 000 — NUMBER 56 (WICKLOW, DUBLIN AND KILDARE)

Most of the route is along a variety of well-defined and interconnecting tracks, paths, trails and forest roads that leave you in no doubt where to place your footsteps. There is one upward section through the pine forest to reach The Spink Ridge where the going underfoot is rougher. Also the paths along the ridge are quite badly eroded in places due to prolonged, heavy usage.

There are adequate signs from the visitor centre to get you to Pollanass Waterfall; after this your navigational skills will be an asset!

GETTING STARTED

The Glendalough Visitor Centre is located off the R757 road, about 2 km ($1\frac{1}{4}$ miles) to the W of the attractive village of Laragh. The centre may be reached from the W by motoring over the Wicklow Gap along the R756 road.

From your parked vehicle, make your way to the visitor centre, which is well worth having an unhurried look around and perhaps even stopping to watch the interesting audiovisual presentation about Glendalough before you explore this for yourself. Afterwards, proceed around the rear of the centre, turning R as directed by the white arrow to pass by the toilet block. Then first veer R to cross over the stream by means of the wooden footbridge to your L. Make your way across the adjacent car park and walk around the rear of the impressive Glendalough Hotel. Turn L to pass through the two stone archways ahead, climbing up steps to do this. You have now entered the grounds of the ancient monastery founded by St Kevin in the sixth century.

ORGANISATION OF WALK AND ASSOCIATED EXCURSION

Providing the weather is fine it makes very little difference in what order you explore the delights of Glendalough and complete your healthy exercise walking along the magnificent heights above the Upper Lake. It is suggested you might start by spending some time at the Glendalough Visitor Centre and then have a first look around the fascinating monastic site. Next complete the walk, or as much of this as you wish to, looking in at the information office *en route* and talking to the helpful staff there if necessary. On the way back you can linger again in the grounds of the monastic site and explore in more detail any of the splendid monuments located there that particularly interested you on the way out.

DESCRIPTION OF WALK

The gateway through which you entered the monastic grounds was probably built between A.D. 900 and 1200, and so, many visitors and pilgrims have already passed this way before you. The tall, round lookout tower is to your R, and directly ahead, beyond the graveyard, are the remains of the large monastery (the Cathedral); both of these fine buildings are well worth examining. Afterwards, continue SW down to St Kevin's Church (or 'Kitchen') with its round, pointed turret. From here, the first glimpses of the fascinations of Glendalough are revealed through the trees on your R.

Proceed through two wrought-iron K-gates and cross over the swiftly flowing Glendasan River by the sturdy, wooden footbridge provided to leave the 'Monastic City'. Then turn R along the wide, gravel-surfaced footpath signed 'Green Road to Upper Lake'. Follow it there. The continuation route leads westwards into the magnificent, steep-sided Vale of Glendalough, a masterpiece of ice sculpture from a previous age. You then pass above the Lower Lake, this nestling in a really tranquil setting down below on your R. Your obvious way threads below feathery larch trees and under the canopy of a mixture of beech, birch and sycamore as you walk right into the open jaws of the glen. The distinctive white backsides of sika deer may often be spotted along this stretch of the way.

Ignore a side path on the R further on, continuing along the main route signed to 'Information Office and Upper Lake'. Then veer R along the lower path to reach the information office, a white-painted building on your R. The staff here are very knowledgeable and will be able to sort out any queries you may have or provide facts that you wish to be aware of about the surrounding landscapes and the flora and fauna that they support.

Turn R from the office to continue W along the glen, where, emerging from the trees, the full grandeur of the middle and upper reaches of Glendalough is progressively revealed. What fantastic sights these are; steep cliffs plunge precipitously down to disappear below the trapped waters that fill the gouged-out upper basin. The steep-sided slopes are partially covered with densely packed trees, but exposed rock buttresses and areas of scree, boulders and shattered rock fragments add to the wildness and awe of this magnificent mountainous setting.

The route continues across the substantial bridge which spans the tumbling waters on your L, but prior to treading uphill along the path ahead, undertake a short detour to inspect the ruins of the Reefert Church and the site of St Kevin's Cell. These are well worth a short visit. After this, start climbing up the wide path leading southwards towards the impressive Pollanass Waterfall. The correct ascent way is above and to the R of these cascading waters. A spectacular, steep-sided, tree-lined gorge is then penetrated, and to get the continued best views of the falls, branch L up the wooden steps keeping to the way signed 'Poulanass Waterfall' (note the slight difference in spelling!). Safe, railed viewing spots have been thoughtfully provided for you to observe the falls. These take the form of several separate plunges, each one disappearing in a cloud of billowing spray into

a dark, deep catchment pool at its base.

Climb above the waterfalls and continue uphill walking SSW veering SW along a well-defined, winding pathway. When this path connects with a wider forest road above, turn L to continue gaining height. However, only a short distance further on, be careful to turn acutely, sharp R off the

⋀ 3:1 ONE OF SEVERAL DEEP CATCHMENT POOLS IN THE POLLANASS WATERFALL SYSTEM

waysigned route and away from the two continuation forest roads which go on to span, by means of bridges, the stream located ahead. The correct way continues up a shallow slope, initially backtracking northwards before it progressively bends quite sharply to the L in a sweeping arc.

Keep progressing along the internal forest road passing by a warning sign that reads 'Danger Cliffs'. Further height is steadily gained as you pass by a rickety stile in the fence on your R. Ignore the narrow path leading off from this but mentally mark the spot, for this is part of your return descent route. Further height is steadily gained as you venture beneath tall conifers and pass by an extensive area on your R where forest harvesting has relatively recently been carried out. Your direction along here is WSW for about 1½ km. Then, past this somewhat desolate area, choose one of several inviting fire-break clearings on your R that pass between the densely packed trees and use the space provided by this narrow opening to climb moderately steeply across the narrow strip of land now separating you from the cliff faces directly above. Your approach to these is northwards, and the way up there is over rough ground littered with twiggy debris.

Quite suddenly you will emerge from the encircling trees to be rewarded by the most fantastic bird's-eye views looking down on rugged Glendalough. Cross over the intervening barbed wire fence with care and turn R to follow the path that snakes above the cliff tops.

The spectacular, quite awesome panoramas to be observed both up and down the glen from along here are sights to be observed for yourself rather than read about in guidebooks! Do just this. As you walk along, the twin lakes of Glendalough are spread-eagled several hundred feet below. Behind, to your L, the glaciated valley rises towards WNW and the main depositor into the lakes, Glenealo River, wriggles about through these wild and barren landscapes.

The well-trodden, cliff-edge path then descends, leading you towards rocky protrusions lining the precipitous fall-away. Keep a close watch on any youngsters in your care along here and take a firm hold of their wrists when passing around the occasional more exposed section! The continuation way undulates eastwards and the eroded ground underfoot can become somewhat boggy along this stretch after heavy rain. Further on, a spur is rounded, and following this the way starts to descend significantly. There are excellent views along the glen from this position, and in clear weather some of the main features of the monastic site may be identified, way beyond the Lower Lake.

Next be vigilant to spot and use a P-stile on the R to cross over the wire fence. Then bear L to continue your descent, now along a narrower, but much drier, grassy path. A steep section down now follows over rough, stony ground and then past a second stile, through a conifer plantation. This part of the way can be slippery when wet so take your time going down and tread with care! Continue descending as the slopes of Derrybawn Mountain put in an appearance to the ESE across the intervening valley.

The path veers to the L towards the bottom of the slope to then adopt a shallower line of descent and, a short distance further on, it connects at that wobbly stile with the forest road you walked along previously. Turn L at this meeting place and retrace your outward steps back to the parking area at the visitor centre, visiting again those sites that particularly interested you or caught your imagination on the way out. If you have time, also walk over to the eastern shores of the Upper Lake where you will be greeted by more superb views up the glorious glen.

SUITABILITY OF WALK AND ASSOCIATED PLACES OF INTEREST FOR FAMILIES

Most family groups will delight in spending time exploring and perhaps picnicking at Glendalough. Those with small children will perhaps not wish to venture beyond the surrounds of Pollanass Waterfall, and it is a delightful walk to get just there. More adventurous teenagers will probably wish to accompany you all the way along The Spink and experience the thrill of walking above those spectacular cliff faces. Take good care of all those in your care along here and, as previously alerted in the walk description, do ensure their safety by firmly holding on to them when you are venturing around the one or two more exposed places!

PLACES OF INTEREST

GLENDALOUGH
More than 500 million years ago Glendalough lay some 500 m (over 1600 ft) below the surface of an ancient sea! Following the 'Big Crash', when the present North American continent ploughed into what is now Europe, molten granite bubbled up to form the Wicklow Mountains. The resultant heat baked the accumulated mud and sandstones thereabout, transforming these surrounding deposits into mica-schist. Later, the sea level fell dramatically and the resulting dry land became arid desert. Prolonged erosion then stripped away much of the schist to expose the underlying granite domes. Finally, during the last two million years (a short period in geological time) successive ice ages brought enormous accumulations of snow and ice to the area, and as the resultant glaciers retreated down the valleys they widened and deepened these, sculpting the spectacular scenery visible today.

▲ **3:2** THE VIEW DOWN GLENDALOUGH FROM THE SPINK

Exploring Glendalough in present times will take you through enchanting landscapes of really outstanding natural beauty. Here you will be able to walk through airy oak woodlands and darker conifer forests, observing at close quarters as you do abundant wildlife and a wide variety of plants thriving in this natural habitat. Red squirrels, peregrine falcons, pipistrelle bats and sika deer are all to be found hereabouts, and in addition to many species of trees and plants, various fungi thrive on the mixed woodland floor where they play an essential early role in converting fallen twigs into fertile soils.

The wilderness and isolation of the area attracted its most famous resident, St Kevin, to found in the sixth century, with a small group of dedicated monks, a monastery on the site. This ecclesiastical settlement flourished and the fame of the holy man spread, attracting many followers and pilgrims to the place. In its heyday the monastery would have included numerous dwellings, workshops, areas for writing manuscripts, guest houses, an infirmary and extensive farm buildings, all these in addition to the usual places of worship. The remains visible today tell only a fragment of this fascinating history and they probably date from between the eighth and twelfth centuries.

Glendalough is now part of the Wicklow Mountains National Park, which was established in 1991 to protect the precious heritage of the area. Excellent information booklets and leaflets on Glendalough are written and compiled by the dedicated staff of this national park, and it is from these and from helpful conversations with the park rangers that much of what is written here has been summarised. This valuable assistance is gratefully acknowledged.

Trooperstown Hill (and Avondale House and Mount Usher Gardens)

fact file

START/FINISH
Village of Laragh — MR 144967

GRADING
Moderate/challenging (colour-coded RED)

WALKING TIME ALLOWANCE
4 hours

DISTANCE
9.7 km (6.0 miles)

TOTAL HEIGHT GAINED
400 m (1310 ft)

HIGHEST POINT
Trooperstown Hill — 430 m (1410 ft)

digest of walk

PARKING
Ample parking on verges and alongside roads near centre of village.

OVERVIEW/INTEREST
- Splendid climb to the summit of a discrete mountain peak.
- Revealing views of the easterly aspects of the high backbone of the Wicklow Mountains.
- Delightful sections through woodlands and forests on the way back.
- Opportunity to visit historic Avondale House and delightful Mount Usher Gardens.

Trooperstown Hill (and Avondale House and Mount Usher Gardens)

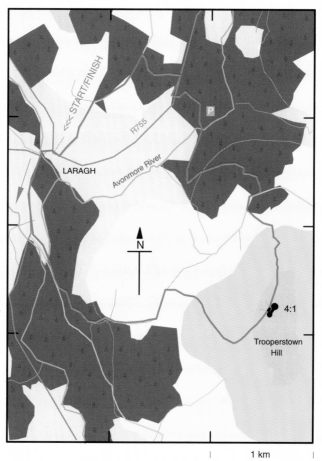

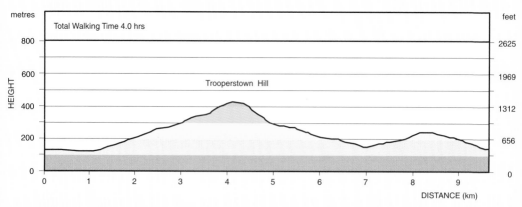

GRADIENTS

Following a section of road walking, there is a steady and continuous pull up to the top of Trooperstown Hill. Fortunately, none of the gradients are too severe and the steeper sections cover relatively short distances. The main part of the descent is quite similar. The final stages of the walk undulate through woodlands and forests, and a downward stretch along a minor road will bring you back into Laragh.

AMENITIES

There is an exceptionally good selection of pubs and restaurants in and around Laragh, and the author has enjoyed sampling several of these!

MAPS, FOOTPATHS AND WAYSIGNS

OS DISCOVERY SERIES 1:50 000 — NUMBER 56 (WICKLOW, DUBLIN AND KILDARE)
The greater part of the route is along an interconnecting network of roads, tracks, paths, quiet back lanes and forest trails encountered in that sequence. Consequently, route finding is reasonably straightforward, but there are a few turnings that are critically important and these are emphasised in the route description. The going underfoot is usually firm and there are few wet spots or stretches of eroded ground.

Apart from along the roads and lanes there are precious few directional indicators!

GETTING STARTED

The attractive village of Laragh, somewhat of a road junction, may be reached from the W along the R756 by crossing over the Wicklow Gap; from Rathdrum to the S along the R755; by motoring from the N along the R115 (old Military Road) by way of Sally Gap; or by using the R755 which leads in from the NE, connecting Roundwood (and, via the R763, Ashford).

From the crossroads in the village centre, select the road signed to Rathdrum (Rath Droma) and walk SW out of the pretty village, passing by Glendalough Forest office on your L. Keep in single file along this relatively busy road where most motorists are not expecting to encounter walkers!

ORGANISATION OF WALK AND ASSOCIATED EXCURSION

You will probably need to set aside two days in order to do justice to the combined delights of Trooperstown Hill, Avondale and Mount Usher. The ideal time to scale Trooperstown Hill is in the morning when the sun is in the best position to illuminate the Wicklow Mountains to maximum effect for you. You may then decide to have a leisurely afternoon before turning your attention the next day to exploring historic Avondale in the morning and the floral wonderland that is Mount Usher Gardens in the afternoon.

DESCRIPTION OF WALK

Follow the road as it veers to the L to head S. When you meet a fork, take the L option to proceed along the minor road. Then, a short distance ahead, use the bridge to cross over the wide, dark waters of the powerful Avonmore River.

Walk past the first track you meet leading off L but follow the second one a short distance further on to walk gradually uphill, immediately passing by an exposed gravel pit. The way forward leads through woodlands and gorse scrub. Higher up, emerging from the trees, pleasant views open up, particularly so to your R and rear. These are of wooded hillsides, with the pointed peak of Paddock Hill visible to the N dominating the surrounding lower landscapes.

Bear L when you come to a junction ahead, still gaining height, now on an eastward bearing. Further on, a spacious and attractively positioned dormer bungalow is approached. Fork R here to pass below and to the R of the bungalow, then heading ENE to ascend some steeper sections of roadway. Higher up, take a peep over the retaining wall on your L to observe in fine weather the valleys of Glenmacnass and Glendasan, the latter snaking up towards the Wicklow Gap. Between these two glens, the higher ground rises progressively to Tonelagee, the huge, rounded peak appearing to the NW.

Just past a venerable old cottage, the track bends sharply to the L and, following this, the upward gradient slackens off appreciably, thus offering a more comfortable rate of climb. Then opposite a gateway on your L, be vigilant to turn off to the R to commence climbing up the open slopes of Trooperstown Hill by walking ESE following a gently rising, rutted way across prickly gorse scrubland. This important turning is at MR 156954. When the track levels off, and just before reaching higher clumps of gorse directly ahead, veer off to the L along a green way. This continues to lead you upwards, now on an eastward bearing.

The fairly obvious, wide track gains further height by means of a series of spacious zigzags that traverse up the

Å 4:1 EARLY MORNING MISTS CLEARING FROM AROUND LARAGH OBSERVED FROM THE TOP OF TROOPERSTOWN HILL
(PHOTO CHRISTOPHER STACEY)

expansive, gently rising hillsides. Progress continues to the SE but then be extra careful to spot and use a relatively obscure, stony track that leads off at right angles on the L, to lead NE more directly in line with the summit. This turning is located at MR 162949 and the narrow path starting from here is not shown on the OS map! Fortunately, the way soon becomes better defined as it bends to the R, still heading upwards. This exceptionally well-drained way then leads fairly directly right to the summit cairn of Trooperstown Hill.

Trooperstown Hill commands a height of 430 m (1410 ft) and in clear weather the all-round views from this rather isolated peak are superb. To the W, extending towards N and S, the high linked peaks and spurs of the distant Wicklow Mountains rise quite spectacularly and a series of deep, finger-like glens infiltrate into this higher ground dividing it up into discrete areas. Consultation with your map and compass will position the many riveting highlights for you amongst this magnificent mountainous terrain. By contrast, the spacious, virtually flat, and quite barren summit area you are now standing on, apart from the man-made cairn, is featureless!

Leave the summit by heading NNE along the obvious continuation, in that direction, of your approach path. The way is now across softer, peat-covered ground. As you start to descend, vast, new lowland vistas open up ahead, these of orderly pastures sprinkled with areas of trees. The path then forks and you must select the L branch. This is the less distinct of the divided ways down. However, within a few paces the narrow path becomes more clearly established as it curves around to the L along a shallow, stony furrow.

The line of descent then steepens for some distance swinging further L, towards and then through N. At the bottom of this steepish slope, continue to bear L, being careful to avoid treading along either a path more directly ahead or another one leading off uphill more to the R! The correct downward direction is now to the NW. This will bring you to a tarmac road below, where you turn R to pass by a quite ugly-looking TV mast. Following an undulating section of roadway and a bend to the R, be careful to select the next turning on the L to pass over a cattle grid before entering Trooperstown Wood.

More height is progressively surrendered as you ignore a branch track off to the R, opting to follow the main forest road that continues to wind downhill. As you descend towards the valley below you will need to avoid more side diversions leading off to both L and R! Lower down, the road performs a hairpin bend to the R to then pass over the Avonmore River by means of a recently constructed, fine concrete bridge. (The previous crossing was swept away by floodwater!) There are more adventurous stepping-stones here, but when last visited these were not complete and the bridge is the only sure way of keeping your feet dry! The internal forest road then rises to connect with the R755 road above.

A THE BRILLIANT COLOURS OF MOUNT USHER'S 'FLOWERING WOODLAND'

Turn R uphill, away from Laragh, but within about 200 paces escape from this busy (and dangerous for walkers!) road, along which vehicles appear to travel at quite unnecessarily high speeds, by turning off L uphill along a more agreeable forest track. This leads W to connect with a minor road above, which you then turn L along. Follow this tarred way downhill for just over 1 km (about ⅔ mile) back into Laragh. The heights of Trooperstown Hill may be savoured again as you complete this final descent, these rising serenely away on your L. The way leads down to St John's Church, and near here a final R turn along the main road will bring you back into the centre of the village.

SUITABILITY OF WALK AND ASSOCIATED PLACES OF INTEREST FOR FAMILIES

The walk is very suitable for older children, most of whom should enjoy the energetic climb to the summit of Trooperstown Hill and thrill from the achievement of getting up there. The climb is probably too strenuous for younger children. However, the delightful attractions of Avondale and Mount Usher Gardens are sure to please young and old alike.

PLACES OF INTEREST

AVONDALE HOUSE AND PARKLANDS

Avondale House, an abode oozing warmth, charm and friendliness, is set in a fine estate of about 500 acres of forest and parkland located along the west bank of the delightful Avonmore River. The site is best known for the fact that on 27 June 1846 Charles Stewart Parnell, one of the greatest and most respected political leaders of modern Irish history, was born here. The great man spent much of his subsequent life at Avondale, and the refurbished house is now a museum dedicated to his cherished memory.

Avondale is also synonymous with the birth and development of Irish forestry. The government purchased the estate in 1904, and it was here that the first experimental plots based on Continental forest gardens were laid out. These plots of about an acre or so can still be seen and enjoyed today. The estate is rich with specimen trees that support a wide variety of wildlife, and as you contentedly walk along under the mature, spreading branches, cross delightful hidden dells and wander along interesting riverbanks, you could spot squirrels, badgers, hares, rabbits and even the elusive otter. The shady grounds are also a bird-watcher's paradise and over 90 different species have so far been spotted at Avondale — see if you can add to this impressive list!

The amenities at this oasis of peace and tranquillity include spacious car-parking areas with adjacent and secluded picnic places; toilets are located in the grounds nearby and there are refreshment facilities at the house. For further information contact:

Avondale House
Rathdrum, Co Wicklow
Tel/Fax: 0404 46111

Coillte Teoranta
(The Irish Forestry Board)
Leeson Lane, Dublin 2
Tel: 01 661 5666
Fax: 01 678 9527

MOUNT USHER GARDENS

The brochure extends a warm welcome for you to visit 'Mount Usher's Flowering Woodland'. This is exactly what it is, 5000 different species of fascinating plants, covering about 20 acres lining the Vartry River, which create a perfect natural harmony between woodland and water that it will be hard to better anywhere. Four generations of green-fingered Walpoles have in fact established one of Ireland's finest gardens from the seeds of the mere potato patch that existed here in 1860.

The author visited the gardens in early May to be greeted with a blaze of rich, vivid colours from the many flowering azaleas and rhododendrons. This feast of gently swaying blooms was breathtaking. Apart from these May-time delights, other ideal times to visit include April when the camellias and magnolias are in bloom; June when it is flowering time for the horse chestnuts and rare tulip trees; July when the lilies and herbaceous plants are at their best; August to see the poppies, buddleias and flame creepers; September to witness the hydrangeas and fuchsias in bloom; and towards the end of September and in October when the maples, berberis and japonicas present a blaze of warm, autumn tints.

Spacious and attractive tearooms overlook the gardens and river, and there is a shopping courtyard that is open throughout the year. Enquiries about the gardens should be directed to:

Mount Usher Gardens
Ashford, Co Wicklow
Tel: 0404 40116/40205; Fax: 0404 40205

OVERLEAF: LOCAL GUIDE MICHAEL DESMOND WITH A GROUP OF WALKERS ON THE CRAGGY KNOCKANAFFRIN RIDGE

NIRE VALLEY
WALKS

NIRE VALLEY WALKS

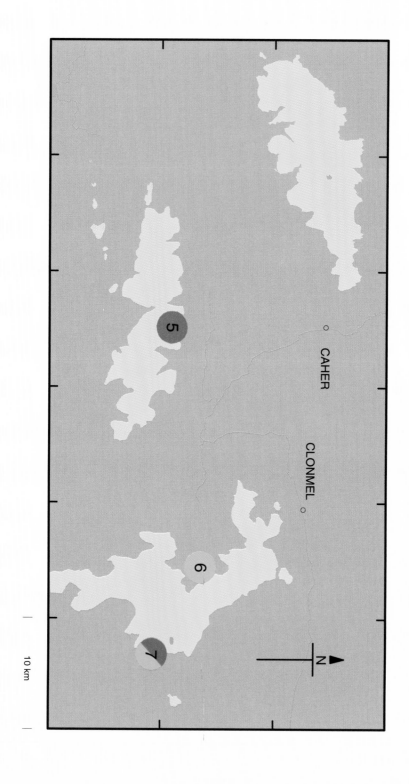

NIRE VALLEY AND THE COMERAGH AND KNOCKMEALDOWN MOUNTAINS

LANDSCAPES AND OPPORTUNITIES FOR SHORT WALKS

The Nire Valley (Nier on OS map) is truly a green and pleasant land. The lower and middle reaches of this meandering vale are liberally covered with woodlands and forests, and the minor roads, trails and paths that criss-cross this area provide countless opportunities for short lowland rambles and nature walks. Higher up, the River Nire penetrates wilder countryside as it drains a great basin stretching upwards towards The Gap and the Comeragh Mountains. Here as well, there are further opportunities for stretching your legs on short strolls that are not too demanding.

The craggy Knockanaffrin Ridge rises to the NW of The Gap and here, the seven separate pinnacles afford other possibilities for short, circular walks in more exposed and exciting terrain. The main plateau of the Comeragh Mountains rises steeply on the other flank of The Gap, towards the SE. This vast summit area contains wild, rough and boggy ground that is too difficult and remote for short walks. However, the rim of this formidable high ground contains a number of spectacular combes, many containing corrie lakes, and getting to these, together with viewing waterfalls cascading down precipitous, rocky gullies, is well within the scope of short walking expeditions.

The massive ridges of the Knockmealdown Mountains rise a short motoring distance to the W of the Nire Valley. Here too, there are ample opportunities for undertaking adventurous, short, circular walks which lead to some of the high points of the ridges and which explore delightful corrie lakes and tumbling watercourses, hidden away in the folds of these huge mountainsides.

Places of Interest Associated with Walking and the Great Outdoors

The area is rich in archaeological sites and many of these may be visited whilst walking in the area. There is also a Cistercian monastery located at Mount Melleray a short distance away by road. However, it is the physical features of the landscapes that are the main attraction in this region. These, in the form of sheltered, wooded valleys and commanding heights rising high above to cradle spectacular, gouged-out combes in which the clear waters of deep corrie lakes nestle, are simply a walker's paradise.

If you do not mind the occasional saunter around built-up areas, then a visit to nearby historical Clonmel, with its medieval origins, gate fortifications, churches, heritage trail and modern shops and amenities, may well be to your taste. Alternatively, you could play a round of golf at the immaculately maintained golf course situated to the SE of the town, although there are those who maintain that this is the most certain way of spoiling a good walk!

For those who do not mind getting sand between their toes, the coast is not very far away, and at Clonea Strand and other nearby places there are vast, sweeping bays and headlands where you can walk for miles without venturing much above sea level. Also, for those who like to combine shanks's pony with being transported about, horse riding and pony trekking are very popular hereabouts and Melody's Riding Stables at Ballymacarbry (Tel: 052 36147) will fix you up with suitable animals for doing just this.

Choice of Walks and Associated Places of Interest

Walk 6 combines a visit to an interesting archaeological site with an exploration of part of the upper Nire Valley. Walk 7 introduces you to the awesome beauty of Coumshingaun Lough nestled amongst the steep cliffs of the Comeragh Mountains. A taste of what the Knockmealdown Mountains have to offer those keen on short rambles is provided by Walk 5, an energetic climb to the summit of Sugarloaf Hill.

WALKING GUIDES, ACCOMMODATION AND EATING OUT

WALKING GUIDES

All my walking with professional guidance in this area has been in the charming company of Michael Desmond, a local dairy farmer whose fame as a congenial and competent leader is now being broadcast far and wide. Michael possesses an encyclopaedic knowledge of these mountains and valleys and he is also an authority on the geology, archaeology, wildlife and flora of this area. He also has a vast repertoire of fascinating stories to tell you, both factual and fanciful!

I have also had the great pleasure of trying to keep up with Seamus Wall and his red setter. Seamus is the acclaimed local 'bog trotter', and he and his charming wife Mary run Hanora's Cottage Guest House located in the Nire Valley. This establishment caters for walkers and more general tourists alike, to whom extremely warm welcomes are extended (see accommodation section below).

CONTACT DETAILS

Michael Desmond
Nire and Comeragh Guided Walks
Deerpark
Ballymacarbry
Via Clonmel
Co Waterford
Tel: 052 36238
Email: hiking@indigo.ie
Web site: http://indigo.ie/~hiking

ACCOMMODATION

The only place we have stayed at in this area, and this now on several occasions, has been with Mary and Seamus Wall at their delightful guest house, Hanora's Cottage, situated near to Nire Church. There is an old saying to the effect that when you have discovered something that pleases you greatly, why change it! This saying certainly applies here. The Walls and Michael Desmond, however, do work in close harmony with a number of other comfortable guest and farmhouses located around the Nire Valley that cater for walkers, and I am sure that you will be well looked after at any place recommended by Mary, Seamus or Michael.

ACCOMMODATION REGISTER

Hotel/Guest House	Rooms en suite		Rooms other		Open
Seamus and Mary Wall Hanora's Cottage Guest House Nire Valley Via Clonmel Co Waterford Tel: 052 36134	F D T S	0 5 3 0	F D T S	0 0 0 0	All year
Paddy and Olive O'Gorman Glasha Farmhouse Four-Mile-Water Via Clonmel Co Waterford Tel: 052 36108	F D T S	1 2 2 0	F D T S	0 0 0 0	All year

Rooms: F = Family; D = Double; T = Twin; S = Single

EATING OUT

Hanora's Cottage Guest House serves the most delicious gourmet dinners, and these together with the delightful surroundings of the cottage make this guest house an almost impossible place to leave during the evenings relaxing there. We have sampled food served on a bed of rice at the Emperor's Palace Chinese Restaurant in nearby Clonmel (Tel: 052 24162) and this is recommended if you enjoy this sort of food. Another alternative, particularly if occasionally you wish to lighten the load on your digestive system, is to sample the value-for-money sandwiches and bar snacks served at Melody's Inn at Ballymacarbry (Tel: 052 36147). However, the main attraction at this popular pub is supping the 'black stuff' whilst trying to catch the sounds of traditional Irish music floating towards you above the lively din during congenial evenings spent there.

SUGARLOAF HILL AND BAY LOUGH (AND MOUNT MELLERAY MONASTERY)

fact file

START/FINISH
Car park near to The Gap —
MR 031100

GRADING
Moderate/challenging (colour-coded RED)

WALKING TIME ALLOWANCE
3 hours

DISTANCE
6.1 km (3.8 miles)

TOTAL HEIGHT GAINED
420 (1380 ft)

HIGHEST POINT
Sugarloaf Hill — 663 m (2175 ft)

digest of walk

PARKING
Large visitor car park located at popular viewing spot on scenic drive; holds about 25 cars.

OVERVIEW/INTEREST
- Energetic climb to the top of a pointed peak.
- Great views in fine weather of both the surrounding Knockmealdown ridges and the distant Galty Mountains.
- The walk incorporates a visit to lovely Bay Lough.

SUGARLOAF HILL AND BAY LOUGH
(AND MOUNT MELLERAY MONASTERY)

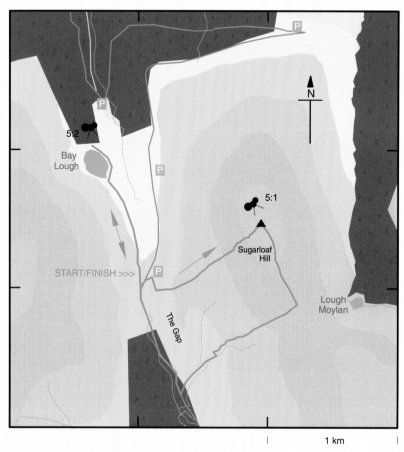

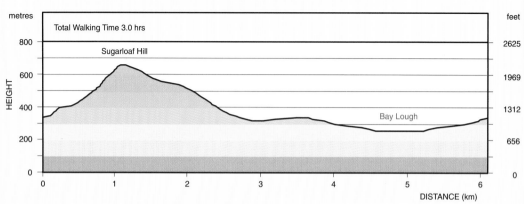

- Chance to pay a visit to the nearby Mount Melleray Monastery.
- Opportunity to taste some delicious local cheese.

GRADIENTS

The walk commences with a fairly steep climb up a rough, eroded path. The longer descent is across more gentle slopes where the going is much easier and relatively effortless.

AMENITIES

None.

MAPS, FOOTPATHS AND WAYSIGNS

OS DISCOVERY SERIES 1:50 000 — NUMBER 74 (CORK, LIMERICK, TIPPERARY AND WATERFORD)

The ascent to the summit of Sugarloaf Hill is up a rough, stony path that is steeply angled. The continuation way along the ridge is clearly defined, but the first part of the descent uses relatively obscure, narrow, connecting paths. These become clearer lower down, and the final section of the walk back to the car-parking area is by the side of the R668 road. The optional extension to reach tiny Bay Lough is along a wide, obvious track. There is virtually no waterlogged ground to cross anywhere.

Signs away from the road and parking area are non-existent but this does not present any significant problems.

GETTING STARTED

The starting-point may be reached from either N or S by motoring along the scenic R668 road. There is a further access road, the R669 that leads NW from Cappoquin.

Once out of the parking area, cross the road and climb the well-used, wide, eroded track that leads up the vast, rough slopes rising steeply to the NE.

ORGANISATION OF WALK AND ASSOCIATED EXCURSION

The complete walk including the saunter to Bay Lough can be completed well within half a day. Choose that part of the day when the weather is likely to be fine in order to complete the walk when the surrounding views are at their best, and fit in your visits to the monastery and to the cheese dairy farm around this priority.

Description of Walk

The walk starts from a lovely scenic spot located in an elevated position on the Tipperary–Waterford boundary. A wide valley falls away to the N, leading the eyes towards the distant skyline where rounded hills rise to culminate in the high peaks of the Galty Mountains to the NW. The much nearer Knockmealdown ridges rise sharply to both W and E, and the slopes of your main objective, Sugarloaf Hill, sweep up from where you stand towards the NE. The statue just above you bears the inscription 'Our Lady of Knock — Pray for us', whilst the two beehive-shaped huts either side of the road formerly were horse-exchange stopping places.

Height is quickly gained as you climb steeply eastwards up the rough, eroded path, and quite soon there are superb views, looking down to your rear, of the place from where you set your footsteps in motion. The tiny, rounded corrie lake of Bay Lough then comes into view, down below to the NNW. For the time being grit your teeth and just keep climbing up, following the obvious, stony way that leads upwards adjacent to walling on your L.

Further up, you have the luxury of a temporary respite whilst walking across a fairly level divide before more energetic climbing is necessary to conquer another steep slope. Take your time accomplishing this, for the main objective of the walk is enjoyment not fatigue! Also, there is wonderful scenery progressively opening up all around you and this is worth pausing for and absorbing in some detail at your leisure. However, some sustained effort will be required to take you to the top of this second pitch.

Then the steepness of the approach slopes gradually declines, and quite often up here a strengthening breeze may be taken as an indicator that you are nearly there! The way up will by now have veered marginally to your L, and after mounting one or two false tops, a final approach along a NE bearing will deposit you on the relatively flattish ground that forms the summit cone of Sugarloaf Hill. The cairn, in the form of a significant mound of stones, marking this high spot lies over to your L.

You are now standing at 663 m (2175 ft) and this is the highest point of the walk. In fine weather you will be rewarded with splendid views from this elevation, including vistas along the undulating continuation ridge that progressively rises, eventually reaching the pointed peak of Knockmealdown, the highest mountain in this configuration. This may be located to the SE. In the opposite direction, the wide, flat lands, through which several tributaries that feed into the River Suir lazily meander, reveal their compelling vastness. Far beyond these green and fertile lowlands the mighty peaks of the Galty Mountains rise to the NW. In the clearest of weather, the shimmering, bluish shapes of the Comeragh Mountains may just be identified far away to the ENE.

A second cairn is positioned just below the summit, and from near here there are more revealing views overlooking Bay Lough. This second pointed landmark is purported to mark the burial place of a certain Major Ely who insisted upon being put to rest 'standing up', with his two faithful hunting dogs and loaded shotgun within reach! This was so that on the final day of judgment he could conveniently just pop down into the woods once more to bag a few pheasants before he permanently rested in contented peace.

Start your descent from the dominant summit cairn, heading S and following the line of the dilapidated boundary walling. The peaty drop down to the wide hause below is shallow to start with, but a short distance further on, it steepens quite abruptly. Here you need to place each of your footsteps with some care, as loose, unstable rock debris litters this part of the path down. Along this section of the way, select a narrow, peat-covered side path that leads off to the L, as this conveniently circles around a more difficult rocky pitch immediately below. The way reconnects with the main path below this obstacle.

Continue to descend towards the hause below, but before reaching the lowest point be vigilant to spot and turn off R along a faint, narrow path, reminiscent of a sheep track, which traverses slightly downhill across the heather-covered slopes. This becomes your continuation way leading down from the spur towards SW. The path becomes better defined lower down as it bears slightly to the R, changing your direction of descent to oscillating between W and SSW. The way down is across vast, open hillsides heading towards the V-nick of The Gap below shaped by a tributary of the Owennashad River.

Lower down you may have to share your descent path with the intermittent use of this by the disciples of motor bike scrambling, the churned-up evidence of which is all too painfully obvious! Continue your descent, keeping to your established westerly bearing to reach a point where another, better defined, stony track joins yours from the L. Use the merged way to track further down, in the process converging with the course of a stream below on your L.

Lower down, the obvious path fans out, presenting you with a number of options. The choice is not critical because these converge again lower down still, all of them leading you the way you want to go. The prolonged descent then connects with the R668 road at MR 033093 just above Glentaunemon Bridge. Turn R up the road to complete the final section of the walk back to the parking area just above.

From the parking area, and after perhaps taking some deserved refreshments, select the wide path that leads off northwards and use this obvious way to walk to Bay Lough below. These tiny trapped waters are less than 1 km ($\frac{2}{3}$ mile) away. The shallow descent there is very pleasant and relaxing, and it gets better still when you reach these cooling waters. Walk around the lough for some distance above its NE shore to obtain the most fantastic view across the waters back up towards The Gap above. Late April or early May is an ideal time to be standing here, when a profusion of flowering gorse will play havoc with the continued conservation of any film that you have left in your camera. Late May will do likewise, with the flowering rhododendrons then being the principal culprit!

SUITABILITY OF WALK AND ASSOCIATED PLACES OF INTEREST FOR FAMILIES

The demanding, steep climb to the top of Sugarloaf Hill will probably be too much for younger children, but should families with such children decide to attempt this they can always turn back if and when the complaints from their young ones become too persistent! Most older children will take the steep slopes literally in their stride and be very pleased with themselves for getting to the top of the challenging mountain.

Sampling the delicious Bay Lough cheeses should be to everybody's taste, whilst the success of a visit to Mount Melleray Monastery will depend on how religious you are and to what extent looking around such holy places appeals to you all.

PLACES OF INTEREST

MOUNT MELLERAY MONASTERY

Mount Melleray Monastery, or Abbey, was founded in 1833 by a small band of hardy Cistercian monks who were presented with a mountainside by Sir Richard Keane of Cappoquin. The monastery is located on the southern slopes of the Knockmealdown Mountains, around MR 097040, and is about 6½ km (4 miles) NW of Cappoquin and about 9 km (5½ miles) from the borders of Tipperary. The grounds and buildings have undergone many changes over the years, and following serious disrepair, the church was extensively refurbished in the early 1980s, when the sanctuary area was redesigned to meet modern liturgical requirements.

There is much to see and to listen to for all visitors who make their way to this great seat of worship and learning. Those pious folk who decide to share a first visit to this religious site with standing on the summit of Sugarloaf Hill will probably wish to return for a longer visit on some future occasion.

BAY LOUGH IRISH FARMHOUSE CHEESE

These delicious cheeses are made from cows' milk with loving care by Dick and Anne Keating of Clogheen, who successfully export their round-shaped product in various sizes to distant lands. The cheese conforms to the standards of the Vegetarian Society, or to be more precise it has reduced fat, less than 2 per cent salt, no artificial colourings, no dreaded E numbers, and for hygiene purposes is entirely wrapped in wax. Flavours of the cheese are also available smoked, using a cold, oak process with garlic and aromatic herbs. Dick and Anne, the dedicated cheesemakers, may be contacted and the cheese sampled at:

Bay Lough Farm
Clogheen
Co Tipperary
Tel/Fax: 052 65275

5:2 TINY BAY LOUGH SURROUNDED BY FLOWERING GORSE IN PROFUSION

Upper Nire Valley
(and Tooreen Archaeological Site)

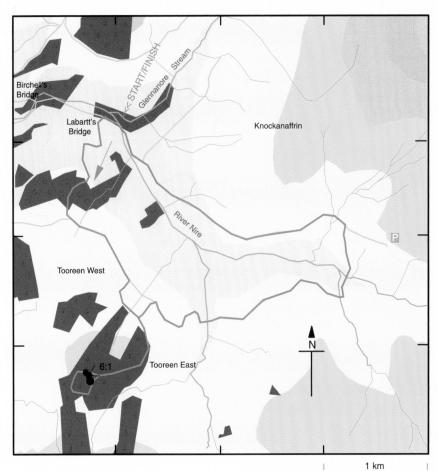

Birchell's Bridge

Labartt's Bridge

Knockanaffrin

START/FINISH

Glennanore Stream

River Nire

Tooreen West

Tooreen East

6:1

N

P

1 km

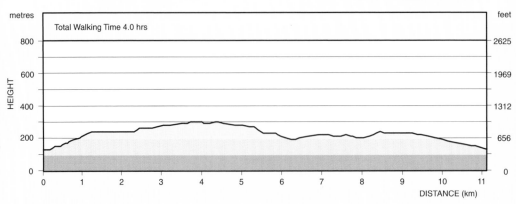

Total Walking Time 4.0 hrs

metres | feet

HEIGHT

800 — 2625
600 — 1969
400 — 1312
200 — 656
0 — 0

0 1 2 3 4 5 6 7 8 9 10 11

DISTANCE (km)

UPPER NIRE VALLEY (AND TOOREEN ARCHAEOLOGICAL SITE)

fact file

START/FINISH
Nire Church and Hanora's Cottage — MR 251139

GRADING
Easy/straightforward (colour-coded BLUE)

WALKING TIME ALLOWANCE
4 hours

DISTANCE
11.1 km (6.9 miles)

TOTAL HEIGHT GAINED
260 m (855 ft)

HIGHEST POINT
Tooreen Archaeological Site — 300 m (985 ft)

digest of walk

PARKING
Limited parking by the side of the road near to Nire Church. (Avoid the times of Mass being celebrated there, for a multi-storey car park might then be helpful to cope with the temporary influx of vehicles!)

OVERVIEW/INTEREST
- Visit to a collection of sites of archaeological significance.
- Excellent views of the nearby Comeragh Mountains.

- Fascinating starting-point from a church, an old school house and an attractive, secluded guest house favoured by walkers.
- Adventurous crossing of a tributary of the River Nire.
- Much to see and absorb for relatively little effort.

GRADIENTS

A moderate slope has to be climbed near the start, and this, with flatter sections, will lead you to the archaeological site above. The walking is fairly easy from here, with gentle downhill slopes for most of the way, these interspersed with a steeper downwards section on a boreen and later a short climb up to a road, this following the crossing of two watercourses.

AMENITIES

By prior arrangement, dinner and refreshments may be booked at Hanora's Cottage Guest House, located at the start of the walk. (See accommodation register on p. 52 for telephone number.)

MAPS, FOOTPATHS AND WAYSIGNS

OS DISCOVERY SERIES 1:50 000 — NUMBER 75 (KILKENNY, TIPPERARY AND WATERFORD)

There are reasonable to good tracks and paths for most of the way and several parts of the route are along minor, surfaced roads. There are also one or two more tricky sections, especially on the way up, where the continuation path and correct way are more challenging to locate.

Signs are few and far between, but some helpful indicators, not yet brimming with information, are provided in the vicinity of the archaeological site.

GETTING STARTED

The upper Nire Valley may be reached from Ballymacarbry to the W by turning off there from the R671 road that passes through the village. There are also scenic approach roads from Clonmel to the NW, departing along the R678 road and then turning off R along either of the two minor mountain roads at MR 248203 or 260203 and heading southwards.

From the vicinity of the church, walk back down the valley road and cross over the gushing waters of the River Nire by the attractive arched bridge. Then turn L along the next broad track and follow the twists and turns of this as it winds quite steeply uphill.

ORGANISATION OF WALK AND ASSOCIATED EXCURSION

Even after allowing ample time to inspect the archaeological sites at your leisure, the round trip may be completed comfortably in about half a day. During the long days of summer the excursion makes a fine evening out.

DESCRIPTION OF WALK

That part of the valley at the start of the walk is fairly steep and narrow and the slopes hereabouts are liberally covered with woodlands. Therefore, initially more distant views are somewhat restricted, and you will need to gain height before the true majesty of the surrounding high mountains is progressively revealed. On the way up, ignore an inviting grassy path on the L, opting instead to continue along the wider way that then passes by a bungalow. You are quite likely to be greeted by barking dogs here, but the agreeable owner will quickly call these to heel once he hears them, and you will find this person also very helpful if you require any expert, local knowledge about the route.

Beyond the bungalow, keep straight on along the obvious continuation path. A short distance further on, the way levels off for some distance as it enters a wooded area. It can also become muddy here! Then continue climbing uphill along a broad, grassy slope, spurning a side path leading off between trees on your R. From near here, the first exciting views of the distant Comeragh Mountains appear in clear weather. The craggy Knockanaffrin ridge and the higher, rounded slopes of the central dome of this uplifted terrain may be identified to the NE and ESE respectively.

Follow the wide, grassy clearing through the trees as it swings around from R to L, still climbing slightly, to pass beneath an electricity cable before you pass by an attractively located dwelling secreted away on your L. Cross over a track leading to this abode to continue uphill along another way that leads off SSW from this important intersection, and then enter another wooded area containing a mixture of ash, birch, hazel, holly and oak trees. The ground below supports lush undergrowth in which bracken and brambles predominate.

Moving on, the surface underfoot deteriorates as a rougher section of stony pathway crosses rutted ground, contorting further uphill. Do not become confused with a tractor track leading off to the R but instead continue straight ahead. After this, a narrower path threads through more open woodlands, heading S and still climbing slightly. Clumps of gorse are passed by, and along here you may encounter more muddy ground churned up by the milling hoofs of cattle.

A further piece of rough ground then has to be crossed, still heading southwards and now walking towards a group of conifer trees positioned directly ahead. This line of approach will lead you to a metal gate, which provides access to the sanctuary of a surfaced lane. Turn L and continue along the fairly level way, walking SE in the general direction of the distant mountains. However, less than a kilometre along the lane, after a shallow descent, branch off along the next narrow track on the R. This important turning, at MR 252125, is opposite a venerable stone barn located just to the L of the road and immediately before reaching a modern bungalow on the R.

A hedged track, grassed over in the centre, then winds further uphill. This is initially to the SW but it then veers SE as the way loops around to the L. It then bends back R again in another shallow arc, reverting to leading you SW once more. This re-established bearing will take you to the archaeological site. Superb views of the wide, open spaces sweeping up to the rugged slopes and undulating skyline of the Comeraghs may be observed from along here in fine weather.

Further on, bear R, maintaining your height by avoiding walking along the grassy track that leads down more to the L. After this, a slight incline leads through a gateway to a parking area that serves the archaeological site, a combination of a stone circle, barrows, stone rows, standing stones and enclosures. The principal features are numbered and there are signed ways that connect them. (A brief description of these features is provided in 'Places of Interest' below, although at present authoritative published information on this site at Tooreen East is scarce.)

Number 1 feature is a stone circle; this is located adjacent to the parking area and is reached by climbing up steps on your L as you approach it. After inspecting it, return to the surfaced area and, as directed by white arrow signs, head up the slope on your R, treading along a defoliated pathway that rises through a sapling conifer plantation to reach a stile conveniently positioned above. Climb this and turn L to walk along the level continuation way that skirts the lower edge of more mature pine and spruce trees. This waysigned track will take you to feature Number 2, which is a barrow and a nearby stone row. Continue from here to then, as indicated by more arrow markers, turn L, cross over a second stile and head back downhill along another defoliated passageway. The descent leads to attraction Number 3, a composite site centred around another barrow. From here, return to the parking area, again aided by helpful directional signs.

Start your circuitous return by initially retracing the final part of your outward route. This is as far as to MR 252122, where you must be vigilant to spot and use the entrance to a partly concealed track that leads down on your R. This important turning is located within an open, grassy area. A steepish section of

⋀ **6:1** PARTLY COVERED STONE CIRCLE AT TOOREEN ARCHAEOLOGICAL SITE

descent then follows along a narrow, constricted, grassy way, your footsteps treading over a rough surface laced with stones and rocks that can become slippery when wet. To add to the frustrations of passing down this funnel, there can also be a preponderance of irritating flies during the summer months!

Fortunately, the connecting path is quite short in length, and you will quickly reach the surfaced road passing by below. Turn R along this more open part of the way and follow the minor road to its terminus about 1½ km (1 mile) further E. However, the road does wind about a bit getting there! This section is downhill and the Glenastuckaun Stream, a tributary of the River Nire, is crossed *en route*, as you walk past several paths and tracks leading off on the R. When the surface underfoot starts to deteriorate, bear around to the R to follow a broad continuation track that will lead you, beneath trees, further E.

A metal gate is then reached, and beyond this bear L to walk downhill, using a wide, grassy path to do so. A stream is then crossed with the aid of stepping-stones. Be careful here, for this crossing can be a bit daunting when the waters are high. Just take your time and only move from one secure position to the next when you are confident about the stride needed to get there. Another metal gate is then negotiated, and through this bear L following the track uphill. Next, pass through a gateway and this leads to a wooden bridge that spans the River Nire, providing a safe and dry crossing of these, on occasions, turbulent, tumbling waters.

After the river crossing, the continuation track leads up the opposite slopes of the wide valley, bending to the L in this process. There are fine, revealing views downstream from here of the contorting upper reaches of the Nire Valley. The track connects with a surfaced lane above, accessed at a padlocked metal gate. Over this obstacle, turn L and follow the narrow, minor road for the remaining 2½ km (1½ miles) of the route back to the vicinity of Nire Church. It is downhill all the way, and all you have to do is consistently ignore side turnings whilst completing this final, straightforward stretch.

SUITABILITY OF WALK AND ASSOCIATED PLACES OF INTEREST FOR FAMILIES

This walk and associated exploration may not be to the liking of younger children. On the other hand, teenagers should enjoy the outing immensely, as they will have an opportunity to combine some healthy outdoor exercise with visiting and inspecting a site of some archaeological significance that will add to their learning.

PLACES OF INTEREST

A very brief description of the three main indicated features of the Tooreen Archaeological Site is provided below. (The name Tooreen probably refers to a drying or bleaching place that was located here.)

NUMBER 1
These are the impressive remains of a circle consisting of 11 stones of various sizes of sandstone conglomerate. The diameter of the circle is approximately 6 m (20 ft) and it is thought that the arrangement of the stones could have some astronomical significance. It is thought that the circle dates from the early Bronze Age, circa 4000 years ago.

NUMBER 2
This site is a barrow (burial pit) with an associated stone row nearby. The row consists of three substantial pointed stones that are aligned on a SSW bearing. The stones are believed to have had some religious ritual significance associated with the barrow.

NUMBER 3
This is a composite site consisting of a smallish barrow, a stone row, a standing stone and a nearby enclosure. Unfortunately, there are indications that this interesting site has been 'grave robbed'.

COUMSHINGAUN LOUGH

factile

START/FINISH

Forest car park — MR 341103

GRADING

Easy/straightforward or moderate/ challenging, depending upon weather (colour-coded BLUE/RED)

WALKING TIME ALLOWANCE

2.5 hours

DISTANCE

4.1 km (2.5 miles)

TOTAL HEIGHT GAINED

290 m (950 ft)

HIGHEST POINT

Just above Coumshingaun Lough — c. 400 m (1310 ft)

digest  walk

PARKING

Attractively screened car park in Kilclooney Wood located just above the R676 road. Room for about 20 vehicles, but with constraining 2 m high entry barrier.

OVERVIEW/INTEREST

- Visit to a gigantic, gouged-out cirque containing a large, very impressive lake.
- Fantastic cliff faces of awesome proportions that plunge almost vertically into the deep, inky depths far below.
- Rock fragments, boulders and loose scree abound.
- Interesting approach through scattered moraine debris.
- Section through woodlands.
- Considered to be one of the finest examples of a corrie lake anywhere in Ireland and frequently visited by geologists from abroad.

COUMSHINGAUN LOUGH

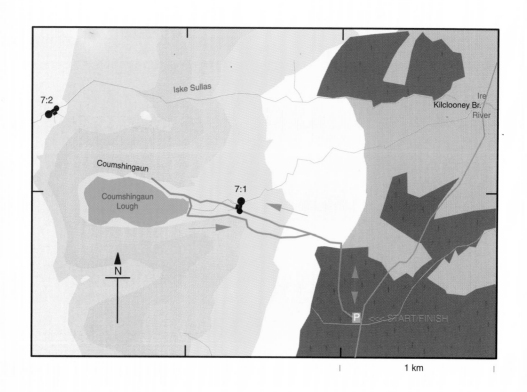

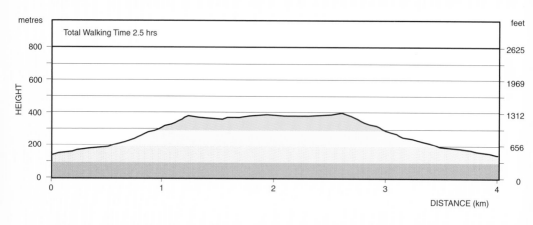

GRADIENTS

Out of the woodlands there is a gradual climb all the way to the lough, but nothing too strenuous. You can weave about whilst gaining height, thus choosing approach gradients that best suit your abilities. The way back downhill reverses this process.

AMENITIES

Picnic places beneath the trees at the parking area.

MAPS, FOOTPATHS AND WAYSIGNS

OS DISCOVERY SERIES 1:50 000 — NUMBER 75 (KILKENNY, TIPPERARY AND WATERFORD)

There are good paths to lead you through the wooded areas. Above the trees, the climb to the lake is across open ground partly covered with gorse scrub and higher up, increasingly littered with stones and rock debris, spilled all over the place. There are some intermittent narrow paths and sheep tracks across these slopes, and the way there is progressively becoming better defined through more and more people using this route from the forest car park to get to the lake.

Away from the vicinity of the parking area there are no guiding signs.

GETTING STARTED

The start of the walk is just off the R676 road. This provides connections to the N with Clonmel via the R678 road and more directly with Carrick-on-Suir; to the S it links with the main N25 route and the coastal fringe around Dungarvan.

Set your feet in motion along the path that leads uphill from the far end of the parking area, immediately passing by an inviting picnic bench.

ORGANISATION OF WALK AND ASSOCIATED EXCURSION

Much will depend on the weather. If you are able to choose a fine, warm, sunny day, make the most of it by setting out early, arranging to have a picnic lunch by the lough, and allowing yourselves as much time as possible to explore and enjoy this unique spot secreted away beneath the steep eastern rock benches of the Comeragh Mountains. Conversely, should you be forced to go there in bad weather, travel light and make a quick 'there and back' of it, during which I am quite sure you will be seduced into wanting to return there sometime when conditions are better!

DESCRIPTION OF WALK

From the start, a wide way winds pleasantly beneath tall Scots pines that for the time being restrict more distant visibility as you penetrate into the depths of the dark forest above. Your narrowing path tracks northwards gaining incremental height to reach more open ground and improved daylight. Hereabouts, beech trees fraternise with the more dominant pines. Further on, the path connects with a wider track running above at a T-junction. Turn R here to maintain your northwards bearing, but in doing so mark this spot well. This is because this important reverse turning is more difficult to find on the way back.

A gentle gradient now leads further uphill threading through clumps of gorse and holly. This part of the way is along a narrow path that bisects sapling pine trees as it maintains a fairly level traverse. Carefully stretch over the wire fence ahead, being mindful that the top strand is of the nasty barbed variety! Then turn full L to continue more steeply uphill using a rougher, stony path that is partly enclosed by dilapidated walling. You should now be heading WNW beside the boundary of the forest, the edge of the trees being on your L. When this boundary swings away further L, abandon it by veering R to cross over a low stone wall that provides access to more open countryside. The rising terrain here is an interesting mixture of intermingled grass and scrubland that contains gorse and boulders.

Work your way up the slopes on a predominately NW to WNW bearing, following what paths happen to lead the way you want to go, seeking out the easier passages through the clumps of gorse and boulders, and outflanking the steeper, more exhausting pitches. Along here, in fine weather, absorbing distant views now begin to open up. Those to the W are the more exciting, as these start to reveal the cragginess of the Knockanaffrin ridge along which jagged rock features proliferate. To your rear, across the attractively wooded, wide valley down below, more gentle contours including those of Croughaun Hill rise more uniformly to the E.

Keep tracking uphill on your established bearing where you should be fortunate to locate better defined tracks, some of which lead your way. Here the going underfoot becomes less exacting although the angle of climb does not abate. Then around the brow of the spur above, given reasonable visibility, your efforts will be rewarded by your first real sights into the massive, gouged-out combe that contains the trapped waters of Coumshingaun Lough. And what a sight this is, particularly so when the upper slopes are partly shrouded in clinging mist which gives the impression that it is rising and that all will be crystal clear when you get there! In any event, impressive rock falls and towering cliff faces will

70

provide an exciting trailer of the delights to come and will inevitably spur you onwards towards them.

Continue to contour around the rising slopes, veering slightly to the L and still gaining height as you seek out whatever help you can from tracks leading you this way. There are many routes through the scattered rocks, boulders and gorse up here and it matters little which one you take providing you do not for the time being surrender any height and you avoid being drawn down to the depressions below on your R, for if you do so, further on you will only have to climb back out of these!

After a prolonged climb, easier slopes of undulating ground are reached and these lead westwards into the recesses of the spectacular corrie. A grassy track of sorts threads a contorting course through a boulder field to get you there, and as you do this, register that you are now walking across glacial debris. Then a small pool is passed and this is particularly photogenic, providing you with a perfect excuse for a short rest! From here, a significantly better defined series of interlinked paths leads further into the embraces of the chasm, still leading you W and still gently upwards.

7:1 KEEN WALKERS MAKING A FAST ASCENT TO THE ROCKY BASIN THAT HOLDS COUMSHINGAUN LOUGH

The rise ahead, best circled around to the R by using a grassy way, is the last obstacle before you reach Coumshingaun Lough. Its setting is simply majestic. You must witness this for yourself to take in its full splendour, as any written words, even those far more eloquent than my own, will prove inadequate to describe its wild, compelling beauty! After you have enjoyed some well-deserved refreshments, there are a variety of paths that circle part of the way around the lake, enabling you to explore further, and to absorb from different perspectives, the superb scenery of this magical lakeside setting. However, do exercise great care when venturing along these mountain paths and do not allow yourselves to experience any exposure that is not to your liking. Be warned: do this by turning back before you reach vantage places that you wish you had not, remembering that often it is easier to climb up than to get down!

For me, the vast scale of the place is one of its most arresting and impressive features. The profusion of rock buttresses, near-vertical cliff faces, jagged pinnacles, fissures, gullies and crevasses which conspire to encircle the lake save for the narrow entrance through which you have just walked, together with its brooding, dark, dramatic waters, even on the sunniest of days, all add to its very special allure. I am confident that all those who venture here will retain a vivid impression of it for ever, one that they will have little difficulty in mentally bringing back into sharp focus whenever they wish to.

To commence your return, initially by a slightly different way, walk back to the point where a small stream exits from the lake, and from here head southwards around the eastern tip of the water. Then before gaining any appreciable height, turn L to locate and follow the lower of several narrow paths that traverse above, around the shoulder of the rising ground now directly ahead of you. This diagonal, a rough, rocky, surfaced channel, climbs away from the corrie, leading you E. The final part of your approach route may now be identified threading through the glacial moraine directly below you.

When the path forks ahead, bear L to start walking downhill. From this decision point use a selection from the multitude of narrow paths and sheep tracks that now wind down along the ridge leading ESE. Lower down, trim your diagonal line of descent to reach the spot where you stepped over the walling near to the edge of the forest on the way up. From here, simply retrace your outward steps, being vigilant to spot and use that important turning, on this occasion to your L, through the trees that you have previously been alerted about.

SUITABILITY OF WALK AND ASSOCIATED PLACES OF INTEREST FOR FAMILIES

Again, allow the weather to be your dominant guide. During fine, warm days at the height of summer, I have witnessed several families with very young children making their way to the lake, with the little ones chattering away and obviously enjoying themselves; later on I have seen these groups relaxing by the lake, mum and dad taking it easy whilst their precious offspring played about under watchful eyes by the edge of the water, this in some carefully chosen, safe spot. Conversely, my wife and I completed this labour of love to Coumshingaun when the weather was quite atrocious and when we didn't see anybody, either on the way there and back, or along the shores of the lake!

PLACES OF INTEREST

COUMSHINGAUN LOUGH

What more can I say! Coumshingaun just happens to be one of the largest and most spectacular corrie lakes in Europe. It is purported to be bottomless and the combe in which it is located is called the 'Valley of the Ants'. In this connection its vastness could probably house all the ants in the world with plenty of space left over to accommodate the odd elephant or two as well! This lake and its setting is one of the most fascinating places the author has ever visited.

OVERLEAF: THE WILD, ROCKY LANDSCAPES OF THE CAHA MOUNTAINS

BEARA
PENINSULA
WALKS

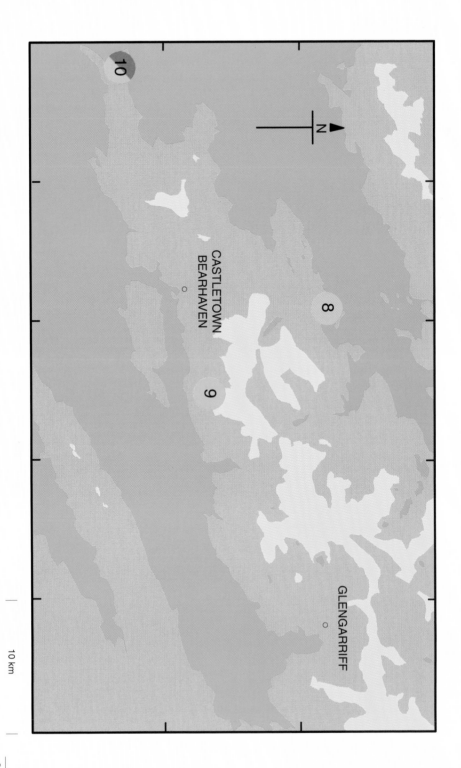

10 km

BEARA PENINSULA

LANDSCAPES AND OPPORTUNITIES FOR SHORT WALKS

Beara is the most remote and least developed of the three major peninsulas that jut out into the Atlantic Ocean in the far southwest corner of Ireland. The high, mountainous spine of the peninsula is composed of tough Old Red Sandstone, and this difficult, craggy terrain, with its formidable access challenges, is, with a few exceptions, out of bounds for short walks.

The coastal fringe, particularly that part towards the western end of the peninsula, does, however, provide many opportunities for short, leisurely walks that are not demanding. Also there are fine walks a short way inland from the coast, part of the way along some of the valleys that wriggle into the higher terrain of both the Slieve Miskish and the Caha Mountains. Bear and Dursey islands also provide further opportunities for stretching your legs over distances that are not too long.

PLACES OF INTEREST ASSOCIATED WITH WALKING AND THE GREAT OUTDOORS

There is a quite superb mountain road that snakes tortuously over the Healy Pass to connect Lauragh in the N with Adrigole to the S, and this adventurous motoring route may be conveniently combined with many short walks located in the more central part of the peninsula. The principal town on Beara is Castletown Bearhaven, which is still an important fishing port. Regular ferries (car and foot passengers) leave from here and nearby for Bear Island. The other main offshore piece of rock, Dursey Island, may be reached by the novel means of being transported high above the waves in a cable car.

The delightful village of Allihies is located towards the western tip of the peninsula, and near here there are the extensive remains of disused copper mines. In recent years this village has become a popular tourist resort in the summer months and during this period these visitors swell the numbers of all-the-year-round walkers. There are also several clean sandy beaches or strands in this area and these are fine for idly strolling along or beachcombing on.

It is apparent that most of the places of interest mentioned are connected with the topography of Beara, for in this region of quite outstanding natural beauty, man-made attractions may be considered to be something of an intrusion into the peace and solitude that walkers are likely to enjoy whilst they are there, at one with nature.

CHOICE OF WALKS AND ASSOCIATED PLACES OF INTEREST

The three short walks chosen are all within easy road distance of Castletown Bearhaven, where the greater part of the accommodation along the peninsula is concentrated. Walk 8 is a walk along the cliff tops north of Ardgroom and this may be conveniently combined with motoring over Healy Pass. A close encounter with the dizzy heights of Hungry Hill just had to be included and this is accomplished by Walk 9, which will lead you around part of Comnagapple Glen. Walk 10 explores the far western tip of the peninsula and provides an opportunity of visiting Dursey Island, providing you are not put off by being suspended high above the swirling seas that often thrash through the narrow sound below!

WALKING GUIDES, ACCOMMODATION AND EATING OUT

WALKING GUIDES

My escorted walking on the Beara Peninsula has been in the agreeable company of either Connie Doyle, a local sheep farmer, or John Gerard O'Sullivan, another farmer who also helps his wife Mary run Sea Villa Guest House situated near Ardgroom. Both these people are expert guides within the areas they know best, namely in the vicinity of Hungry Hill for Connie and around Ardgroom for John. Both will divest interesting local knowledge to you as you walk along and point out features of interest that are passed by. Connie may be contacted through the proprietors of either of the first two guest houses listed in the accommodation register below, while John is included in the fifth such listing there.

ACCOMMODATION

We have stayed with Ann and Teddy Black at their comfortable guest house 'Seapoint', which is conveniently situated just outside Castletown Bearhaven, and also with Helga Savage, just along the road at 'Island's End'. You will be made most welcome and well looked after at either of these establishments where members of the walking fraternity are especially favoured. Ann is keen on the outdoor life, and she and her husband will act as your knowledgeable walking consultants whilst you stay there. Helga will make sure that you are never thirsty, although remaining on your feet whilst partaking of this hospitality is entirely your own responsibility!

ACCOMMODATION REGISTER

Hotel/Guest House	Rooms en suite		Rooms other		Open
Ann Black Seapoint Castletownbere Beara Co Cork Tel: 027 70292	F D T S	0 2 2 0	F D T S	0 0 0 0	March to Oct
Helga Savage Island's End Rossmackowen Beara Co Cork Tel: 027 60040	F D T S	0 0 0 0	F D T S	0 2 2 1	All year
Ford Rí Hotel Castletownbere Beara Co Cork Tel: 027 70379	F D T S	0 0 17 0	F D T S	0 0 0 0	All year
Michael and Mary Donegan Realt na Mara Castletownbere Beara Co Cork Tel: 027 70101	F D T S	2 1 1 0	F D T S	1 0 0 0	All year
Mary and John O'Sullivan Sea Villa Guest House Ardgroom Beara Co Cork Tel: 027 74369	F D T S	0 3 1 0	F D T S	0 0 0 0	April to Oct
Paddy and Agnes Sheehan Windy Point Guest House Garnish Beara Co Cork Tel: 027 73017	F D T S	3 1 0 0	F D T S	0 0 0 0	April to Oct

Rooms: F = Family; D = Double; T = Twin; S = Single

EATING OUT

By arrangement you can have dinner at either 'Seapoint' or 'Island's End'. Castletown Bearhaven and the larger town of Kenmare have a range of restaurants, cafés, pubs and hotels to suit most tastes and purses, whilst the renowned Lawrence Cove Seafood Restaurant (Tel: 027 75063) on Bear Island operates an inclusive ferry service from the mainland as part of the evening out. Two unpretentious eating places that we have tried and enjoyed very much are Murphy's Restaurant and Jack Patrick's Restaurant, situated close to one another in Castletown Bearhaven.

PULLEEN LOOP NEAR ARDGROOM
(AND HEALY PASS)

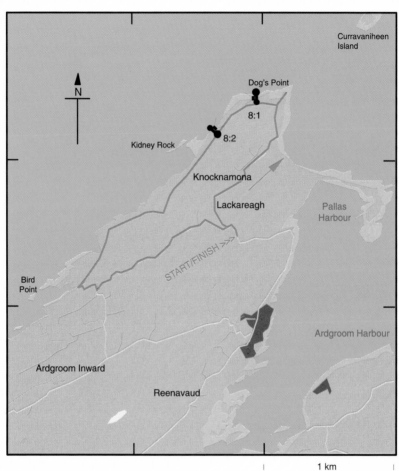

Curravaniheen
Island

N

Dog's Point

8:1

Kidney Rock

8:2

Knocknamona

Lackareagh

Pallas
Harbour

START/FINISH

Bird
Point

Ardgroom Harbour

Ardgroom Inward

Reenavaud

1 km

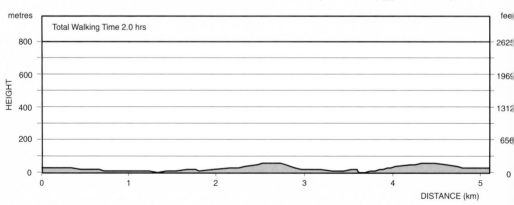

Total Walking Time 2.0 hrs

PULLEEN LOOP NEAR ARDGROOM (AND HEALY PASS)

fact/ile

START/FINISH
Sea Villa Guest House, Ardgroom — MR 698575

GRADING
Easy/straightforward (colour-coded BLUE)

WALKING TIME ALLOWANCE
2 hours

DISTANCE
5.1 km (3.2 miles)

TOTAL HEIGHT GAINED
140 m (460 ft)

HIGHEST POINT
Along the rocky coastline at a place called Mullach — 65 m (215 ft)

digest o/walk

PARKING
Space for about 10 cars at Sea Villa Guest House; seek permission from the helpful owners John and Mary O'Sullivan to leave your vehicle there. (John may even be prepared to act as your paid guide!)

OVERVIEW/INTEREST
- Superb coastal scenery viewed along a rocky headland.
- Caves and other rugged rock features out to sea.
- Pleasant, rural inland landscapes.

- The way passes through tiny hamlets and by a number of farms.
- A section of the Beara Way is used.

GRADIENTS

There are fairly gentle ups and downs for much of the way, but none of these slopes are particularly challenging.

AMENITIES

None, apart from at the guest house by prior arrangement.

MAPS, FOOTPATHS AND WAYSIGNS

OS DISCOVERY SERIES 1:50 000 — NUMBER 84 (CORK AND KERRY)

The start and finish of the walk use quiet back roads and minor lanes. Along the coastal section of the route there are a number of narrow paths that are becoming increasingly well trodden and route finding presents minimum difficulties. There are few boggy areas, apart from the approach to Dog's Point early on.

This walk is being further upgraded by the enterprising Beara Tourism & Development Association, and, where most needed, extra stiles and more waysigns, additional to the marker posts already in position, will add to the overall attractiveness of this route, particularly for casual walkers.

GETTING STARTED

Use the R571 road that links Castletown Bearhaven with Kenmare to reach the tiny village of Ardgroom. Turn off N at the village to travel along the western shoreline of Ardgroom Harbour, where at the quay the narrow lane turns inland to bring you to the starting-point for the walk just a short distance further on, up a turning on the R.

Walk back down the entrance drive to the guest house, turn R along the lane below and you are on your way.

ORGANISATION OF WALK AND ASSOCIATED EXCURSION

This delightful, short coastal walk, which is full of interest, may be conveniently combined with a circular tour that takes in the adventurous crossing of the Healy Pass, motoring over the narrow mountain road that bisects the high ground of the Caha Mountains.

Allow a full day for this fascinating adventure and try to choose one when visibility is good so that you can absorb the many-splendoured mountainous vistas at their best. The power-assisted part of the circuit may be undertaken in either direction and the walk commenced near the time you happen to be passing through the village of Ardgroom.

DESCRIPTION OF WALK

The walk starts from a fairly remote part of the northern coastline of the Beara Peninsula where rugged, rocky scenery abounds. The land rises to the SE in the shape of the undulating, craggy spurs denoting the mountain chain of Coomacloghane. These formidable slopes form the distant horizon in that direction. Opposite to this, green pastures dotted with small farmsteads occupy a low-lying valley that quite naturally leads the eye NW across the intervening bay towards the far-away, shimmering skyline of the high mountains of Iveragh.

Veer R along the lane comprehensively signed 'Lascaireacht — Beara — Shore Angling — Trá — Strand (Beach)'. (An additional waysign for walkers is planned to be positioned here!) You should now be proceeding NW along a narrow, hedged lane, heading directly towards the coast. Following a slight rise, the lane swings round to the R and from along here the most majestic seascapes come into view, including those across indented Ardgroom Harbour and towards the headland more directly ahead.

⚊ 8:1 PAUSE FOR BREATH WHILST CLIMBING KNOCKNAMONA

A small stream appears down below filling a cleft on your L and this is crossed further on as the lane swings round in that direction. A sign denoting the 'Beara Way' (this is a long-distance walking route) is then passed and near here bear L, keeping to the lane and ignoring a side route straight ahead. (Note: This side turning leads to Pulleen Strand where an alternative parking area serving the walk is currently being developed.) The continuation way then bends acutely L, climbing slightly. However, within 50 paces or so branch off the surfaced lane to the R to follow the signed way across rough, rocky ground, making good use of a faint, narrow path.

The continuation way, which does become wet and boggy in places, necessitates the crossing of a tiny watercourse as it threads uphill, leading you northwards through a mixture of brambles, gorse and heathers. Higher up, the path becomes better defined as an attractively located bungalow is passed by to your R, and at the top of the rise beyond this you will reach a black marker post. As directed, turn R here to then head directly towards Dog's Point further on to the NNE. The next marker post is slightly to the L, and from here continue northwards, passing by more posts and weaving about slightly to avoid further squelchy ground, to reach the headland of Dog's Point. Waves crash over the layered rocks down below here and this is a favoured spot for deep-sea fishing.

⚊ 8:2 THE RUGGED COASTLINE PROTECTING ARDGROOM HARBOUR

Retrace your steps back along the headland to reach the last marker post again and from here head SW, keeping the cliff faces a safe distance to your R! The correct way is indicated by another marker post off to your L. From here, the ground rises gently snaking through a soft carpet of heathers and low-lying gorse. Continue SW hugging the attractive coastline to pass by a further post that identifies the continuation of the Beara Way. Your elevated route then passes by Bionn na Carraig, which means 'The Place of the Rocks'. These are to be sighted down below on your R in the form of inclined bedding planes that rise just above the surface of the sea, causing white water to continuously break over them throwing cascades of spray high into the air.

The faintly defined path continues to track between SW and WSW along the knobbly ridge passing close by more helpfully positioned marker posts and eventually a small cairn is reached. This marks the highest point of the walk at 65 m (215 ft) and this place is known locally as Mullach. Here, on this exposed, often breezy, platform, you may feel at one with nature, revelling in the openness of the magnificent panoramas that surround this idyllic spot. In fine weather you should be able to identify the start of the walk to the ESE from here.

Start descending, with the cliffs still close on your R, to pass by further posts that mark the continuation of the Beara Way and also more positions from which deep-sea fishing is popular. The ensuing descent is prolonged but gradual and there are more fine views as you surrender height, these of the attractive coastline stretching directly ahead, further to the SW. Below, you will soon reach a small cove formed by layered bedding planes of rock. Turn L here as directed, to then carefully descend down a craggy cleft as the Caves of Cuas come into view directly below, across the swirling, frothy waters that constantly swill into their gaping mouths.

Circle above these awesome openings in the cliff faces, following a narrow, adventurous path where you must be cautious to ensure that each step you take is secure! Turn L again when you reach the next marker post to traverse down a rocky section of the path to reach the security and shelter of the inland cove below. Often when gales are blowing, seaweed, volumes of it, is washed up through the cave systems by the pounding seas, and this slippery flotsam then needs to be crossed to reach a wooden ladder stile which has to be climbed to access the continuation way. Following this, the way leads gently uphill over a second stile to reach Cuas Cove where a small pier has been built.

Cuas Cove is another picturesque inlet that usually contains moored fishing boats and their assorted tackle. A narrow lane winds uphill from the cove and you exit along this way, heading back E. Turn L when you reach the T-junction ahead and after looping over the hillside beyond, the return journey descends to pass by several farmhouses, one of which is sheltered by palm trees! A short distance further on you will reach the turning off to the L that you branched off along near the start of the walk. On this occasion, ignore the turning, instead continuing along the lane to arrive back at the entrance drive to Sea Villa.

SUITABILITY OF WALK AND ASSOCIATED PLACES OF INTEREST FOR FAMILIES

The walk is not too strenuous or difficult to navigate along and as such will suit most family groups containing older children. However, the way does traverse an exposed, rocky headland with one exacting drop down near to the Caves of Cuas and, therefore, it is not considered suitable for your beloved young ones!

The drive over Healy Pass should appeal to all the family and those with young children who decide upon undertaking this adventure could split up for the walk. Adults in charge of the tiny tots might walk a short way along the last section of the route or even as far as Cuas Cove and the fishing boats to rendezvous there with the rest of the family who undertook the complete walk.

PLACES OF INTEREST

HEALY PASS

The Healy Pass is the high point of an adventurous mountain road (R574) that tortuously snakes through a gap in the Caha Mountains, linking Lauragh to the N with Adrigole to the S. This high-level connection, less than 10 km (about 5 miles) in length, crosses through superb mountainous terrain, and in particular the views taking in Glanmore Lake and those along the valley of the Glanmore River surrounded by the high peaks of Lackabane, Eskatarriff, Knocknagree, Hungry Hill and Coombane must rank amongst the very best in the whole of Ireland.

Work on the road commenced during the famine years in 1847–8 but was abandoned due to a combination of the high death rate and inadequate finance. Development restarted in 1928 at the instigation of Tim Healy, the first Governor General of the newly formed Irish Free State and a native of Bantry, hence the name of the pass. The road was finally completed in 1931.

A well-stocked gift shop is located at the top of the pass and the nearby Crucifixion Shrine was erected there through the generosity of an anonymous donor in 1935. These buildings stand at a height of about 300 m (985 ft) at a point on the border between Cork and Kerry.

COMNAGAPPLE GLEN CIRCUIT (AND BEAR ISLAND)

fact file

START/FINISH
Parking space adjacent to R572 road — MR 745474

GRADING
Easy/straightforward (colour-coded BLUE)

WALKING TIME ALLOWANCE
3 hours

DISTANCE
7.2 km (4.5 miles)

TOTAL HEIGHT GAINED
230 m (755 ft)

HIGHEST POINT
Rossmackowen Commons — 240 m (785 ft)

digest of walk

PARKING
Limited parking area with space for only four or five cars. Additional private parking ground further up the lane; seek permission to use this if necessary.

OVERVIEW/INTEREST
- Adventurous, low-level circuit below the towering bulk of Hungry Hill.
- The route passes close by a profusion of awesome rock features.
- A visit to the reeded waters of tiny Park Lough.
- Open landscapes for most of the way, with views of sweeping coastal scenery, including Bear Island.
- A section of the Beara Way is used.
- Abundance of bird-life, including jackdaws.

COMNAGAPPLE GLEN CIRCUIT
(AND BEAR ISLAND)

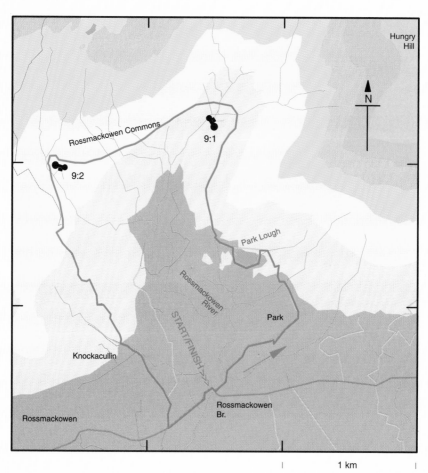

Hungry
Hill

N

Rossmackowen Commons

9:1

9:2

Park Lough

Rossmackowen
River

START/FINISH

Park

Knockacullin

Rossmackowen
Br.

Rossmackowen

1 km

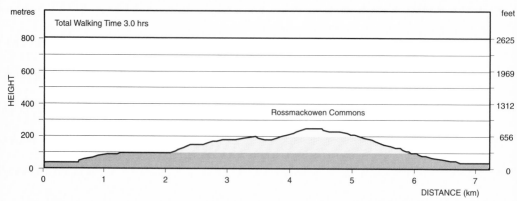

GRADIENTS

There is an easy, gradual ascent first into and then traversing along part of Comnagapple Glen to reach the high point of the route at Rossmackowen Commons. From here it is mostly downhill with the steeper slopes located towards the start of the descent.

AMENITIES

None.

MAPS, FOOTPATHS AND WAYSIGNS

OS DISCOVERY SERIES 1:50 000 — NUMBER 84 (CORK AND KERRY)

The start and finish of the walk are along lanes, wide tracks and a section of the R572 road, approached in that sequence. In between these, there is a mixture of narrow tracks and paths of varying degrees of clarity but some open ground has to be crossed. However, there is never much doubt about which way to proceed.

There are helpful waysigns near the start and along the significant section of the walk that follows the Beara Way.

GETTING STARTED

Travel along the scenic R572 coastal road to reach the parking area near to Rossmackowen Bridge. This is located about midway between Castletown Bearhaven and Adrigole, close to a distinguishing hairpin bend.

From just off the main road, make your way up the side lane heading NE towards the jagged, craggy, westerly spurs of Hungry Hill.

ORGANISATION OF WALK AND ASSOCIATED EXCURSION

Complete the walk in the early morning if you can, leaving the rest of the day free to visit and spend as much time as possible on nearby Bear Island.

DESCRIPTION OF WALK

The lane winds pleasantly uphill passing between high hedgerows that contain assorted flora, including honeysuckle and fuchsia. The route then bends around to the L, gaining further height, and from this elevated vantage point the hilly, elongated shape of Bear Island may be studied as it comes into view below you on the far side of Bear Haven. Given good visibility you will also be able to spot part of Sheep's Head Peninsula stretched out beyond the island. Your progress changes to NW, and past a metal gate as you veer further L you will reach the placid waters of Park Lough. Venture around these to the L, or seaward side,

leaving the wide path and traversing across wetter, rougher ground along a narrow track to achieve this.

In summer, this tiny, reeded lough attracts plenty of bird-life, whilst marginal plants thrive along its shallow, boggy shores. At this time of the year water lilies tend to cover its limited surface area as trout swim undisturbed below. From the far side of the

9:1 Crossing Comnagapple Glen beneath Hungry Hill

trapped waters there is a splendid view across the lough towards the steeply rising crags of Hungry Hill, and this alone justifies your temporary departure from the relative comfort of the wide path! You will need to veer R off the approach track and climb up a craggy rise near to the water's edge to obtain the best photographs of the lough.

Complete the circuit around Park Lough by returning to the main cart track and turn L along this to continue on your way. Your heading is initially NW across fairly level ground before you start to swing around to the R as the route twists and turns below a formidable jumble of rock benches that tumble down on your R in awesome profusion. These are the start of a rocky ridge that climbs steeply towards the vast summit area of Hungry Hill, high above to the NE.

Then the ground ahead starts to rise more steeply as your way curves progressively, further to the R. From here, the wide, green track that you are using snakes into and then along the R-hand flank of a wide, glaciated valley below on your L. This is named Comnagapple Glen, which means 'The Cwm of the Horses'. You have one guess to name which animals previously grazed on these slopes! The far side of the gouged-out basin is flanked by another bristly ridge and the narrow apex of this forms part of the boundary line between Cork and Kerry.

Marker post number 53 of the Beara Way is then passed, and beyond this the route continues NE passing through really spectacular mountainous scenery where more of the craggy, westerly features of Hungry Hill are revealed. Gentle undulations follow as you penetrate deeper into the upper reaches of this remote and sublime valley, and from along here you may position the tiny, secluded cottage, visible in clear weather to the WNW, where the author and historian Hugh Lee wrote his books in splendid isolation.

Marker post 54 comes and goes and more height is gradually attained before flatter ground is eventually reached. The ground then falls towards a small but fast-flowing mountain stream, and here you turn L as indicated by the adjacent waysign (presumably post 55 but this was not marked as such when last visited). From here, track downstream now progressing W and heading for the footbridge below. After passing by marker post 56 use the wooden, railed bridge to cross above the rocky bed of the stream. A less-well-defined part of the way leads further downstream from here, crossing over some patches of rather boggy ground.

Continue westwards past post 57, first surrendering more height as you hug the rock benches rising on your R before taking a slight rise in your stride to reach post 58. More soggy ground lies ahead as you continue to contour around and then climb up grassy slopes that stretch towards steeper, rockier ground above. In this process you pass by post 59 to then reach post 60. This last marker indicates that, now standing at 240 m (785 ft), you have reached the highest point of the walk along Rossmackowen Commons, and it is nearly all downhill from here.

Bear L from this high spot and descend along a narrow, rocky gully. The way down quickly widens into a grassy channel that threads between rock faces. A small stream is crossed and more boggy ground has to be taken in your stride before you reach post 61. From here, the route leads further W for a short distance, rising up another grassy slope to rendezvous with post 62. Turn sharp L here to head down steeper slopes, then tracking S across rough, rocky ground.

A wider stream has to be crossed as you strike a beeline for post 63, which is located just below a large sheep dip. After this, continue to traverse around the hillside along a narrow but clearly defined path to pass by a solitary hawthorn tree. Your descent upgrades to a green road before post 64 is passed and beyond this marker there is another gentle uphill section. Then you should be able to spot standing stones both ahead and down below on your R. These mark burial places.

The way down then leads to a T-junction where post 65 is positioned. You depart from the Beara Way at this point, doing so by turning downhill to the L. A wide cart track provides the continuation way as it winds gently down southwards towards the coast below. Further on, raise the looser part of a wire fence that stretches across the track to duck beneath it and then avoid a side turning leading off on the L. This is shortly before you connect with the R572 directly below. Turn L here and use the road to cover the remaining short distance that will return you to your starting-point.

Suitability of Walk and Associated Places of Interest for Families

This walk is considered to be eminently suitable for most families, apart perhaps from those with tiny tots who are too big to be papoosed. Virtually everybody should be able to make it to Park Lough, and carrying fishing nets with the anticipation of using these is usually the right incentive for encouraging smaller children to make their way up rising ground without too much complaining!

Places of Interest

BEAR ISLAND

This strip of hilly land lies just off the southern coast of the Beara Peninsula opposite the fishing port of Castletown Bearhaven and it is separated from the mainland by the narrow straits of Bear Haven. The island is some 10 km (about 6 miles) long and has a width of just under 3 km (nearly 2 miles). The green, rounded hillsides of Knockanallig rise to 258 m (845 ft) marking the highest elevation on the island, and just below this, on the summit of nearby Coomastooka, a massive white cross has been sited to mark Holy Year 1950. This testimony bears the simple inscription 'ERECTED BY THE PEOPLE OF BERE ISLAND AT HOME AND ABROAD'.

The main village is Rerrin, located towards the eastern tip of the island, and there is a ferry service from here across Bear Haven to the mainland at Beal Lough. There is also a renowned eating place at Rerrin, the Lawrence Cove Seafood Restaurant (Tel: 027 75063), which not only specialises in serving delicious fish dishes but also operates an inclusive ferry service between the mainland and the island as part of the

⋀ 9:2 THE GENTLE SLOPES LEADING DOWN TO THE COAST FROM ROSSMACKOWEN COMMONS

evening out. An alternative, more frequent and significantly shorter car and passenger ferry crossing links Castletown Bearhaven with the western end of Bear Island.

Should you be in the vicinity of Rerrin and wish to stretch your legs, walk the short distance westwards along the quiet road to admire the superb view down along the tiny creek of Lawrence's Cove across the intervening straits towards distant Hungry Hill.

GARINISH STRAND AND BALLAGHBOY (AND DURSEY ISLAND AND ALLIHIES)

fact/ile

START/FINISH
At or near to Garinish Pier — MR 522428

GRADING
Easy/straightforward to moderate/ challenging, depending upon the weather (colour-coded BLUE/RED)

WALKING TIME ALLOWANCE
2.5 hours

DISTANCE
5.7 km (3.5 miles)

TOTAL HEIGHT GAINED
210 m (690 ft)

HIGHEST POINT
Above Ballaghboy — 151 m (495 ft)

digest o/walk

PARKING
There is space for about 15 cars near the pier at Garinish. (This is just past the post office, where you will find Pat O'Neill very helpful.)

OVERVIEW/INTEREST
- The walk starts from a tiny, picturesque harbour.
- Superb coastal scenery all the way around the route.
- Revealing views of nearby Dursey Island.

GARINISH STRAND AND BALLAGHBOY
(AND DURSEY ISLAND AND ALLIHIES)

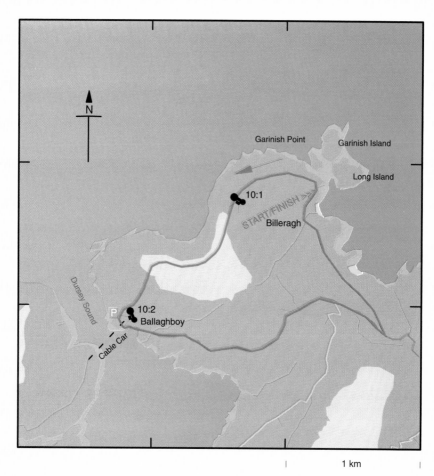

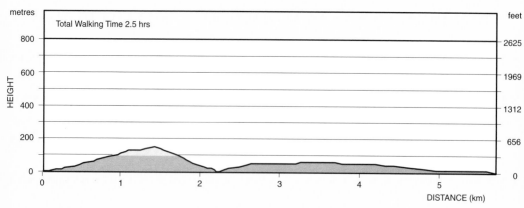

- Rugged coastline with cliff faces, sheltered coves and sandy beaches.
- Opportunity to visit Dursey Island and nearby Allihies.
- Route follows part of the Beara Way.

GRADIENTS

There is a prolonged pull up from sea level towards the high point of the walk. Then, following some undulations, it is mostly downhill, at first across fairly steep, grassy slopes and then along minor roads where the gradient in places is almost imperceptible. There is one other uphill section just after the Cable Car Station.

AMENITIES

See what the post office at Garinish has to offer! There is also the Cable Car Station serving Dursey Island and, during the summer months, an attractively located café is open at Windy Point Guest House near the Cable Car crossing.

MAPS, FOOTPATHS AND WAYSIGNS

OS DISCOVERY SERIES 1:50 000 — NUMBER 84 (CORK AND KERRY)

The walk utilises a mixture of paths, tracks and sections across open, uncharted hillsides followed by a descent along connecting minor, surfaced lanes and roads.

The walk is well indicated by waysigns and marker posts and there are directional road signs once you reach the roadways.

GETTING STARTED

From Castletown Bearhaven travel westwards along the R572 coastal road and remain on this route until you finally reach the turning off on the R towards Garinish. (This turning is just after you have passed through Firkeel Gap.) You can also reach Garinish from the NE by travelling through Allihies along the R575, but this is a more tortuous approach along a narrow, twisting road.

From your parking spot, walk NW past the jetty slipway and continue along the grassy track above the shoreline as directed by the waymarker.

ORGANISATION OF WALK AND ASSOCIATED EXCURSION

If possible, complete the walk during a morning when only light winds are blowing. This will leave the rest of the day free to visit the associated attractions of Dursey Island and Allihies, or to relax on one of the nearby sandy beaches. Alternatively, on a fine, sunny day, consider undertaking the walk in the late evening in order to be in a position to observe the magnificent sunsets that often appear along this stretch of coastline.

DESCRIPTION OF WALK

Spectacular coastal scenery surrounds the starting-point of the walk, which is from just above a tiny, sheltered harbour where an assortment of colourfully painted, small boats bob about on the waves, straining at their mooring ropes. Beyond this, across the wide, sweeping bays to the NE, the rugged, undulating shape of the Knocknagallaun–Knockoura ridge provides an arresting horizon.

Proceed through the metal gate and walk uphill towards the marker post above, crossing over a small stream to get there. Continue up the grassy slopes, now heading more directly W for a stretch before you start to circle L, and then aim towards the craggy high point visible in clear weather on the far horizon. A narrow path leads in this direction threading through a series of rocky outcrops. The next marker post is soon left behind and from here, the correct route ahead and the position of the next marker may be identified. These will confirm that you need to continue tracking upwards on a WSW bearing, taking the gentle undulations along the way in your stride.

The next marker post is located on a rocky mound and points you SW directly towards the high ground above. Vast, panoramic views abound from this vicinity given clear visibility, of which those to your rear down across Garinish Bay are quite supreme. Some wet, boggy ground lies ahead, and in getting around this be particularly careful not to lose your sense of direction. This is because the next marker post indicating the correct, negotiated way across this privately owned land is slightly off to the L and you will need to head SW to locate and reach it. (Note: My wife and I had the good fortune to meet Francis P Sullivan, who grazes sheep on these grassy slopes, and he very helpfully pointed us along the straight and narrow hereabouts. I am sure he will do likewise for you should the need arise and you have the good fortune to spot him herding his woolly flock with the aid of his faithful sheepdogs.)

From here, the hillsides above angle up more steeply, but this is compensated for by this higher ground, covered by an attractive mixture of heathers and gorse, being better drained. These upper slopes are accessed through a gap in a section of ancient stone walling marked by another post. A narrow track then leads further up the massive hillsides leading directly towards the pointed rocks that form the interesting skyline above. You still need to head SW up this steeper gradient. Maintain this established bearing to pass by the next marker post, climbing diagonally along a faint, grassy path and refraining from turning off this way along any of the numerous sheep tracks that circle around the mountain and bisect your way up as they do so.

Eventually, the summit rocks come within reach, but to get there you will need to climb a high ladder stile. This is positioned over to your R. Safely over,

△ **10:1** Tackling the sweeping lower slopes of Ballaghboy above Garinish Point

climb up the grassy knoll above, from where there is a fantastic view of the near-vertical cliff faces below. Another marker post indicates the continuation way from here, as more fantastic seascapes appear. These include the raking headland jutting out to sea to the SSW that culminates in Crow Head and Crow Island.

The onward route is then along a craggy ridge that fortunately has a benign, rounded, grassy apex which provides safe and easy passage. Another ladder stile is crossed, after which the obvious way continues along the ridge, passing by more marker posts. From along here the pointed Skellig Rocks may be seen, piercing dramatically through the waves to the NW. Then you will have the thrill of your first sightings of part of nearby Dursey Island. During the following gentle descent, more revealing views of the island appear, including those of the narrow straits that separate this gigantic chunk of rock from the mainland.

A well-established section of path leads down the next headland, skirting beside a wire fence to lead you past another marker post. The high point of these headlands is marked by yet another post, this one set in a plinth of concrete. Turn L at this point to pass by a tiny cairn and continue descending west to south-westwards aiming directly towards Dursey Island. A faint, grassy path will then lead you down to another ladder stile that needs to be crossed. A clearer path tracks further downhill from this point, heading directly towards the Cable Car Station below and dropping down quite steep slopes. There are alternative descents and the marked way keeps to the higher ground of the rocky ridge for some distance further before leading down along a shallower slope. The choice of ways here is entirely yours.

Whichever descent you choose, on the lower ground head for the marker post positioned above a tiny cove. This important sign marks the crumbling edge of an eroded cliff face that has been sensibly fenced off. Keep well away from this hazard and head along the coastline to pass by the next marker post and access another stile. You will now have reached the parking area serving the Cable Car Station where you will spot an interesting signpost informing you 'Moscow 3310 Km — New York 5280 Km'. Once again, the choice is yours!

Assuming you do not intend sampling the adventurous crossing to Dursey now, head E uphill along the winding, tarmac-surfaced road where the only hazard to watch out for is inconsiderate traffic! You will soon reach Windy Point bungalow where a café is open during busy periods, and this could well add some time to how long it takes you to complete the rest of the walk. From here, more delightfully located homesteads line your return and, over a gentle rise ahead, it is downhill all the way to reach the road junction at MR 527418, less than 2 km (about a mile) further on.

On arriving at this junction, ignore the side lane leading off on the R along which the Beara Way continues, and instead turn L along the minor road comprehensively signed to 'Garinish Pier — Trá Garinse — Garinish Beach'. The final part of the descent is to the NW and this will lead you directly back to the spot where you abandoned your vehicle earlier in the day. Several sheltered coves and some fine, sandy beaches are passed by *en route*, and these might also delay your return.

🔺 **10:2** A BIRD'S-EYE VIEW OF DURSEY ISLAND

SUITABILITY OF WALK AND ASSOCIATED PLACES OF INTEREST FOR FAMILIES

The walk is suitable for families with older children, but because of the prolonged climb up to and the degree of exposure along the craggy headlands, those with small children are advised not to undertake the entire walk. The associated activities and places of interest should appeal to all, and, given fine weather, toddlers and those who also do not wish to walk very far should have little difficulty enjoying themselves on one or more of the fine, sandy beaches located nearby.

PLACES OF INTEREST

DURSEY ISLAND

Visitors to Dursey will discover an island of spectacular beauty and a haven of relaxing tranquillity. It is reached from the mainland by travelling, perched in a cable car, high above the waves of the dangerous, intervening straits. This is the only one of its kind in Ireland. The cable car is said to hold either up to eight passengers or one cow! It operates on Mondays to Saturdays, weather permitting, between the hours of 9 to 11 a.m., 2.30 to 5 p.m. and 7 to 8 p.m. (For Sunday crossings telephone 027 73017.)

The highest point of the island lies at 252 m (825 ft) and a Martello lookout tower is located here. In addition, from various other elevated vantage points, there are fascinating sightings of the offshore rocks, The Bull, The Cow, The Heifer and The Calf. Many rare sea birds may also be spotted from these lookout places.

ALLIHIES

The attractive village of Allihies overlooks picturesque Ballydonegan Bay with its fine strand and clean, sandy beaches. The small village is now a popular holiday resort with several pubs and restaurants, a significant assortment of comfortable bed and breakfast and self-catering establishments, and a number of hostels. There are also campsites and a riding centre.

In the nineteenth century this remote village came into prominence as the setting for Ireland's most extensive copper-mining industry, which at its peak employed up to 1200 people. The evidence of this industrialisation remains above the village, where dilapidated steam-engine houses with their tall chimneys, other mine-related buildings and the extensive spoil heaps will readily conjure up, for those interested, visualisations of the toil and sweat that were part and parcel of recovering the copper ores from deep below ground and of then processing and refining these valuable extracts.

Iveragh
Peninsula
Walks

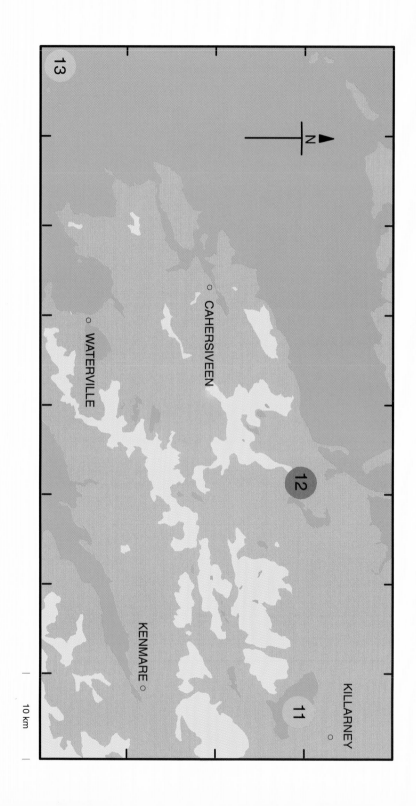

KILLARNEY LAKES AND IVERAGH PENINSULA (RING OF KERRY)

LANDSCAPES AND OPPORTUNITIES FOR SHORT WALKS

To many people, the mere mention of the words 'Killarney Lakes' will immediately conjure up visions of breathtaking countryside, this filled with spectacular mountain peaks, wooded valleys and tranquil lakes, jogging carts clicking along quiet country lanes, friendly people who will pass the time of day with you, and a place where the mere movements of the hands of a clock matter little.

Walkers intent on short walks in this wonderland of nature will not be disappointed with such preconceived images. When they get there they will discover that away from the hustle and bustle of Killarney town as they explore the magnificence of Killarney National Park they will become encapsulated within a reality of natural beauty that if anything surpasses its fame. Here, visitors have a mouth-watering choice of short walks, ranging from lakeside strolls, following nature trails through deciduous woodlands and tramping through conifer forests to scaling modest hills and venturing part way up formidable, high mountains. Waterfalls may be visited *en route* and there are ample opportunities for wandering through parklands and formal gardens.

The rugged landscapes of the Iveragh Peninsula stretch away to the W of Killarney National Park, and these in the form of the MacGillycuddy's Reeks contain the highest mountain in Ireland, Carrauntoohil. Although it is not suggested you venture into any of these high places on a walk planned as a short one, it is surprising what may be achieved by modest hikes into the valleys surrounding these mighty peaks. For example, short walks into or through the Gap of Dunloe, along the lower reaches of Hags Glen or to the northern shores of Coomasaharn Lake will lead you to superb viewing places where you will be surrounded by fantastic, craggy mountain peaks soaring up high above you.

There are countless further opportunities for short walks along the coastal fringe of the peninsula, and these include exploring craggy headlands and wandering across sandy bays and strands. These become prolific towards the western extremity of Iveragh, where they include exploring the offshore landscapes of Valencia Island and perhaps even scaling the steps that wind up the steep, rocky slopes of Great Skellig.

PLACES OF INTEREST ASSOCIATED WITH WALKING AND THE GREAT OUTDOORS

Apart from the many attractions of the tourist lollipop of Killarney town with its hotels, shops, eating places, museums and so on, the Iveragh Peninsula contains an abundance of places of interest and things to do that may be conveniently combined with short walks.

On the shores of Lough Leane you will be able to inspect Ross Castle, and dotted around the higher Muckross Lake are Muckross House and Gardens, the Meeting of the Waters, the Old Weir Bridge and Torc Waterfall. Further upstream are Lady's View and Moll's Gap, both quite superb vantage points. For those who enjoy floating on water, there is a variety of boat cruises on Lough Leane and elsewhere, and more modest craft may be hired for fishing trips etc. Cycling is also very popular, particularly along the flatter forest roads and bridle-ways. Bird spotting and nature rambles are also here in abundance.

In Iveragh, much of interest rightly belongs to the awesome topography of the landscapes, but two other major attractions are the Kerry Bog Village Museum located between Killorglin and Glenbeigh and the Skellig Heritage Centre just across the water on Valencia Island. A visit to the wonders of the glaciated Gap of Dunloe will have almost universal appeal whether you walk through this cleft in the mountains or allow horses to carry your weight.

CHOICE OF WALKS AND ASSOCIATED PLACES OF INTEREST

Exploring part of the famed Lakes of Killarney is catered for by Walk 11, which will lead you around Ross Island and provide you with the opportunity to stand on the ramparts of the castle located there. The other two routes will lead you progressively westwards, into and then beyond the Iveragh Peninsula. Walk 12 is an exhilarating climb to the top of Seefin combined with a visit to the Kerry Bog Village Museum which is located in the shadow of this fine mountain, while to complete Walk 13 you will first need to travel across the waves to disembark on Great Skellig.

WALKING GUIDES, ACCOMMODATION AND EATING OUT

WALKING GUIDES

I did not use local walking guides to sort out the fairly obvious walks I undertook around the Killarney Lakes. However, whilst exploring the Iveragh Peninsula I had the pleasure of walking on several occasions with young, local guides employed by 'Go Ireland'. This is a well-established and enterprising walking organisation based in Killorglin that offers a wide range of inclusive walking tours, guided walks and assistance to independent walkers. The guides of 'Go Ireland' that I walked with were really professional, and apart from making available their skills and knowledge of the area, they were great fun to be with and they were very competently able to combine safety with enjoyment. Two other organisations in the area offering walking tours and so on are 'Countryside Tours' and 'Into the Wilderness Tours', although I have not so far walked with either of these enterprises.

CONTACT DETAILS

Go Ireland
Old Orchard House
Killorglin
Co Kerry
Tel: 066 9762094
Freephone from UK: 0800 371203
Fax: 066 9762098

Countryside Tours Ltd
Glencar House
Glencar
Co Kerry
Tel: 066 9760211
Fax: 066 9760217
Email: country@iol.ie

Johnny Walsh
'Into the Wilderness Tours'
Climbers' Inn
Glencar
Co Kerry
Tel: 066 9760101
Fax: 066 9760104
Email: climbers@iol.ie
Web site: http://www.iol.ie/~climbers

ACCOMMODATION

Through introductions kindly made for us by a combination of the Killarney Tourist Office and the three walking organisations mentioned above, we have had the pleasure of staying at several friendly hotels and up-market guest houses in the Killarney and Iveragh region. Without exception, all of these places (listed below) have an empathy towards walkers and their needs, and you will receive a warm and friendly welcome at each of these establishments, together with enjoying comfort and eating a delicious, hearty breakfast each morning before you set out.

ACCOMMODATION REGISTER

Hotel/Guest House	Rooms en suite		Rooms other		Open
Tim Buckley Glena House Muckross Road Killarney Co Kerry Tel: 064 32705; Fax: 064 35611	F D T S	4 10 10 2	F D T S	0 0 0 0	March to Nov
Teresa Clery Slieve Bloom Manor Guest House Muckross Road Killarney Co Kerry Tel: 064 35055/34237	F D T S	10 3 0 0	F D T S	0 0 0 1	All year
Abbie Clifford Clifford's B&B Waterville Co Kerry Tel: 066 9474283	F D T S	3 2 1 0	F D T S	0 0 0 0	March to Nov
Tommy and Kay Woods Park House Laharn Killorglin Co Kerry Tel: 066 9761665	F D T S	2 0 0 0	F D T S	1 1 1 0	March to Oct
Glencar House Hotel Glencar Co Kerry Tel: 066 9760102	F D T S	2 4 9 3	F D T S	0 0 0 0	All year
Johnny and Anne Walsh Climbers' Inn Glencar Co Kerry Tel: 066 9760101 Fax: 066 9760104	F D T S	3 9 0 0	F D T S	0 0 0 0	March to Nov plus Christmas/ New Year

Rooms: F = Family; D = Double; T = Twin; S = Single

EATING OUT

You will be spoilt for choice in Killarney, and Waterville, towards the other extremity of the area covered, also boasts a wide variety of places where you can eat your fill at a price to suit your pocket. There are also gastronomical delights to be discovered in between these two locations.

Some of the various eating places where we have enjoyed a wide range of meals and considered these represented good value for money whilst touring around the area include: in Killarney, Paddy's Restaurant (Tel: 064 36600) and the Allegro Family Restaurant (Tel: 064 32481); near the Gap of Dunloe, Kate Kearney's Cottage (Tel: 064 44146); in Killorglin, Bianconi (Tel: 066 9761146); near Glenbeigh, the Red Fox Inn and Restaurant (Tel: 066 9769184); and in Waterville, An Corcán (Tel: 066 9474711) and the Sheilin Seafood Restaurant (Tel: 066 9474231).

Ross Island and Castle (and Killarney)

fact file

START/FINISH
Ross Castle car park — MR 951889

GRADING
Easy/straightforward (colour-coded BLUE)

WALKING TIME ALLOWANCE
2.5 hours

DISTANCE
6.5 km (4.0 miles)

TOTAL HEIGHT GAINED
50 m (165 ft)

HIGHEST POINT
20 m (65 ft)

digest of walk

PARKING
Extensive parking facilities in two separate areas. However, these quickly fill up at popular visiting times.

OVERVIEW/INTEREST
- Enjoyable walk through dense woodlands skirting the shores of Lough Leane.
- Plenty of bird-life and other forest creatures.
- Good views across the lough towards Tomies, Shehy and Purple mountains.
- Visit to a castle stronghold dating back to the fifteenth century.
- The relics of a copper mine may be inspected.
- Opportunity for a boat trip.

ROSS ISLAND AND CASTLE
(AND KILLARNEY)

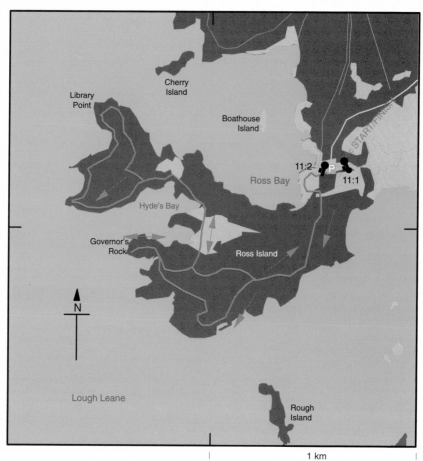

1 km

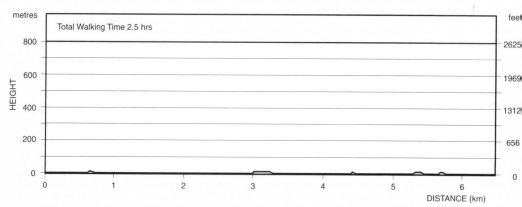

GRADIENTS

Virtually none.

AMENITIES

Refreshments, a shop and toilet facilities are located near the castle.

MAPS, FOOTPATHS AND WAYSIGNS

OS DISCOVERY SERIES 1:50 000 — NUMBER 78 (KERRY)

NATIONAL PARK SERIES 1:25 000 — KILLARNEY NATIONAL PARK

A combination of surfaced ways, wide paths and forest trails that are adequately signed make route finding undemanding.

GETTING STARTED

Ross Castle is located on the shores of Lough Leane, about 2 km (just over a mile) to the SW of the centre of Killarney. Leave the town along the main N71 motoring (or walking) S. Just past a major roundabout be vigilant to turn R by the side of a petrol station, to then proceed past the golf links cum racecourse down to one of the parking areas located near the lake.

From either parking area, walk down towards the lake and castle, the tower and turrets of which are visible directly ahead above the tops of the screening trees. Venture inside the castle or walk around it if you wish to save this delight for later.

CAUTIONARY NOTE

When the waters of Lough Leane are high, they tend to flood over parts of the low-lying strips of land that provide access to some of the most westerly protrusions of Ross Island. In these conditions, assuming you are not wearing waders or are not keen on paddling in bare feet, the walk as described may need to be curtailed!

ORGANISATION OF WALK AND ASSOCIATED EXCURSION

The combined walk and visits to the associated places of interest may be completed in any particular order that suits you. However, if you are not staying in the town, allow the best part of a whole day to complete the walk, to have a look around Ross Castle, perhaps to have a sail on Lough Leane, and to shop in and sample the gastronomic and other delights of Killarney.

DESCRIPTION OF WALK

There are fine views from the boat jetty in front of the castle across the expansive, lapping waters of Lough Leane. These are SW towards the high peaks of Tomies, Shehy and Purple mountains, rising steeply above densely wooded, lower slopes. Continue past the jetty area to then walk by the boat yards, following a narrow path that winds around these to the L. At the T-junction ahead, turn R along the tarmac-surfaced road, walking S into the deciduous woodlands stretching beyond.

From here, the way snakes gently upwards, in the summer months through quite dense, overhanging foliage. Further on, be careful to spot and turn off down a narrow side path on the L. The next section of the way soon broadens out to a lovely walk just above the shore of the lough, threading through a pleasing mixture of trees, bushes and copious ground foliage. An attractive, wooded dell is then crossed where you need to bear R, thereby avoiding a stub path leading off to the L. This will connect you with the next part of the route, which is along a narrow, grassy path that threads through bracken.

Another wooded dell is passed, after which the path swings around to the R, becoming broader and better defined as it returns you to the roadway again. Turn L and after about 50 paces along the surfaced way, bear L at the fork ahead to continue in the direction signed 'Governor's Rock'. From here, the continuation way winds gently downwards to present you with a further choice of ways. Again veer L to come to the attractive shore of the lake once again, where you continue along a raised causeway that bisects small pools cut off from the main lake. The remains of copper mines are there to be discovered and examined in this vicinity.

Continue westwards along the wide, curving way that is also popular with horse riders. Keep to the main path as it curves upwards to the R to bring you to another intersection of ways. Turn L here, to then head towards Governor's Rock and Library Point. From here, the way is downwards through tranquil surroundings where only birds singing and the crushing of your boots break the silence of the woodlands. Then a short distance further on turn L along the side path again signed 'Governor's Rock'. This is in fact an impressive, tree-covered knoll with a rocky edge falling into the waters of Lough Leane, from which further arresting views across the lake may be absorbed. A picnic area is located here and the place is purported to have earned its name from the fact that the headman, who was called 'The Governor', liked to spend time at this spot. (Unfortunately, the way there may be one of those areas cut off by the high water level in the lough.)

Return to the main track and turn L to continue your winding way beneath the trees, for a short distance eastward. Then turn L along the track signed

'Library Point 1 km'. (Here again, access ahead may be cut off in the Irish monsoon season by surface water having spilled from the main lake into low-lying pockets of ground and this could thwart your intended progress.) Unless impeded by surface water, your continuation way will lead you through a pleasing mixture of open spaces and enclosed woodlands *en route* NW to the headland beyond.

This wooded area may be explored at your leisure, as more fine views across Lough Leane appear through a succession of gaps through the trees. There are a series of interconnecting paths hereabouts and you may circle around the promontory. Doing this, you will reach a craggy spot known as 'The Library'. Again there is a good reason for this particular name being chosen, because the rock formations here resemble a pile of huge books. It is said that when the wind blows from the NW the motions beneath the water appear to turn the pages of these images over. (The author has also heard other 'Old Fishermen's Tales'!)

11:1 ROSS CASTLE ON THE SHORES OF LOUGH LEANE

After exploring the headland, return along the kilometre or so back to the junction with the main track. On this occasion, turn L to commence, as indicated by the sign there, your return to the vicinity of Ross Castle, now some 1.1 km ($\frac{2}{3}$ mile) away. This will provide a pleasant ending to the short, undemanding stroll as the route passes through more mixed woodlands that contain an assortment of beech, birch, bracken, hazel, hawthorn, rhododendron, rowan and Scots pine. Along this stretch, keep to the main surfaced track by bearing L when you come to the junction ahead and then passing by the side loop off to the R that you used on your outward route.

SUITABILITY OF WALK AND ASSOCIATED PLACES OF INTEREST FOR FAMILIES

The walk and the associated places of interest are eminently suitable for most families of all age groups and if you are content to be constrained by keeping to the main, macadam-surfaced paths, you may be enticed to push a buggy and its precious contents along with you as well.

PLACES OF INTEREST

ROSS CASTLE

Ross Castle may be considered to be a typical example of the stronghold of an Irish chieftain during the Middle Ages. The O'Donoghue Ross clan built it probably in the late fifteenth century. The barrack alongside dates from the mid-eighteenth century. Now restored, the castle houses a fine collection of sixteenth- and seventeenth-century oak furniture. Access is by guided tour only and the incentive to join one of these is that the several level, stone fortifications contain, amongst other rooms, a private parlour, a justice room, a guard room, a musicians' gallery, a great hall and a bed chamber.

For details of opening times, entrance charges and other information, telephone 064 35851.

⋀ 11:2 LOUGH LEANE AND THE HIGH MOUNTAINS FLANKING THE GAP OF DUNLOE

SAILINGS ON LOUGH LEANE

There are a variety of boating opportunities available from the various piers located near Ross Castle, including the private hire of fishing boats. Many visitors will opt for a cruise on the spacious *Lily of Killarney* watercoach, which is an ideal and relaxing way of viewing part of the Killarney National Park whilst you absorb the live commentary provided.

Reservations for the cruise may be made by contacting any of:

Killarney Boating & Tour Centre (Tel: 064 31068)
Dero's Tours (Tel: 064 31251/31567)
Killarney Tourist Office (Tel: 064 31633)

BOATING TOURS INCORPORATING THE GAP OF DUNLOE

The Gap of Dunloe Boating Tour, operated by O'Donoghue's, has long been recognised as one of Killarney's premier and most scenic full-day outings. The cruise begins from the western tip of the Upper Lake at a lovely spot named Gerrameen. The boat will then take you through the Three Lakes of Killarney, down The Long Range River, past the Meeting of the Waters, under Brickeen Bridge and across the largest lake, Lough Leane, to your disembarkation point at Ross Castle.

For further information or to book your passage, contact:

O'Donoghue's Boating Tours
Old Weir Lodge
Muckross Road
Killarney
Co Kerry
Tel: 064 35593/33483
Fax: 064 35583

KILLARNEY

Killarney town with its magnificent lakes and surrounding mountains is world famous, attracting visitors, some of whom return many times, from distant lands. This major tourist centre has appropriate accommodation to suit all tastes and budgets, this ranging from luxurious, 5 star hotels to simple hostels. A wide range of shops cater for both everyday necessities and expensive, luxury presents, whilst your appetite and thirst may be satisfied in a great variety of pubs, cafés and restaurants that serve most things between fast-food and gourmet meals. Other indoor attractions include a number of art galleries, a library, a hotel leisure centre open to the public, a children's activity centre and a museum of Irish transport.

Killarney is always busy to overflowing during the main holiday season, when you are advised to book accommodation, reservations at restaurants and your favourite seat in the pub of your first choice well in advance. The town is not exactly the quietest of places at all other times either!

SEEFIN
(AND KERRY BOG VILLAGE MUSEUM)

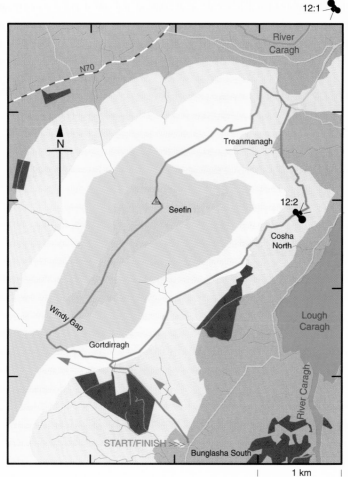

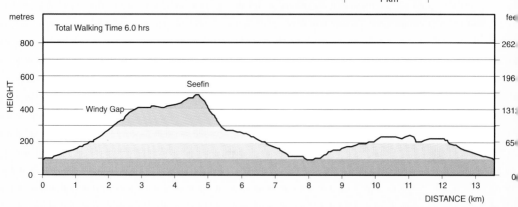

SEEFIN (AND KERRY BOG VILLAGE MUSEUM)

fact file

START/FINISH
Park near to Bunclash old school house — MR 692872

GRADING
Moderate/challenging (colour-coded RED)

WALKING TIME ALLOWANCE
6 hours

DISTANCE
13.5 km (8.4 miles)

TOTAL HEIGHT GAINED
590 m (1935 ft)

HIGHEST POINT
Seefin — 493 m (1615 ft)

digest of walk

PARKING
Space for about eight cars along a side lane used by the Kerry Way long-distance walk. (This area is directly in front of a bungalow and be courteous not to obstruct the entrance drive here.)

OVERVIEW/INTEREST
- Energetic climb to the top of a superbly located mountain peak.
- Revealing views of the westerly aspects of the famed MacGillycuddy's Reeks.
- Fantastic seascapes out towards and across Dingle Bay.
- Plenty of wet, boggy ground to test your resolve!
- Route uses sections of the Kerry Way.
- Opportunity to visit nearby Lough Caragh and the Kerry Bog Village Museum.

GRADIENTS

There is a gradual pull up to Windy Gap, and from here steeper slopes sweep up towards the vast summit areas of the broad ridge above, culminating in the summit of Seefin. The first part of the descent is steeper still, across loose surface ground where in places it is a challenge to retain your balance. These gradients decline lower down, and the final sections of the walk are across undulating slopes followed by a gentle walk down, retracing your initial outward steps.

AMENITIES

None.

MAPS, FOOTPATHS AND WAYSIGNS

OS DISCOVERY SERIES 1:50 000 — NUMBER 78 (KERRY)

There are significant sections at the start and finish that follow surfaced lanes and wide tracks. Between Windy Gap and your descent to Treanmanagh the ground is rough and there are only sections of fairly faint, intermittent, narrow paths to guide you. The approach to Seefin from Windy Gap crosses extensive areas of poorly drained ground where surface water and boggy areas present serious challenges!

There are no signs other than those along sections of the Kerry Way that skirt around and below the higher ground. Cairns are also few and far between, although there is a substantial pile of stones, together with a trigonometrical point, located at the summit of Seefin.

GETTING STARTED

The start of the walk is a few kilometres S of the village of Glenbeigh, which is on the main N70 coastal road that forms the famed 'Ring of Kerry' motoring route. The starting-point is best reached by turning off the N70 and then using the minor roads to travel along the western shores of beautiful Lough Caragh. Your stop is about a kilometre to the SW of the southern tip of the lake, just after passing Bunclash old school house.

Those staying in Glencar may reach the starting-point direct by travelling NW along the minor roads signed to Lough Caragh.

From your parked vehicle, proceed uphill along the surfaced lane as directed by the Kerry Way sign. Your initial heading is N veering NW directly towards the gap in the rounded hillsides rising above.

ORGANISATION OF WALK AND ASSOCIATED EXCURSION

Let the weather determine the sequence of your standing on top of Seefin and absorbing all that the bog village museum has to offer. Should the weather be fine when you arrive in the area, make the most of it by lacing up your walking boots right away, leaving the delights of inspecting cottages from a bygone era until later in the day.

DESCRIPTION OF WALK

You are immediately surrounded by vast, open spaces, and mountain peaks of all shapes and sizes encircle you. Lord of these heights are the fantastic, pointed peaks of the distant MacGillycuddy's Reeks soaring up to the ESE and culminating in the cone of Carrauntoohil, at 1039 m (3410 ft) the highest place in Ireland. For the time being you may concentrate on absorbing this magnificent scenery, for your continuation way is obvious as it winds gently uphill along a broad track.

Your main objective, the summit of Seefin, rises to the NNW, but for the time being this is obscured by the rounded contours of the vast approach slopes beneath it. Ignore a side track off to the R before a conifer plantation is passed by and where more side exits need to be avoided. If you are walking this route in either April or May, colourful gorse thickets are then bisected. More turnings off to both R and L need to be spurned until you come to a choice of ways at MR

12:1 SEEFIN RISING SEDATELY ABOVE GLENBEIGH

682882. Be careful to turn L here, to continue up rising ground along a green way. (However, mark this spot well, for the track leading more directly ahead but then bearing R that you have spurned is in fact part of your return route.)

Pass through the metal gate, beyond which a wide, stony path winds gradually up to the top of the broad hause that separates the Seefin ridge from the slopes rising to Beenreagh to the SW. For fairly obvious meteorological reasons, the top of this pass is named Windy Gap. Just before you reach the apex of the col you will pass by a wooden stile on the L, and a few paces further on, locate and turn off along a narrow, rocky path that traverses up the mountainside on your R, changing your heading to E veering NE.

This path becomes more difficult to follow higher up and in places it peters out altogether. However, keep to your established NE diagonal, making towards the higher ground and threading across slopes covered with a mixture of grass, heathers and stones, following a continuation route of your own choice. This approach will lead you on to the broad apex of the ridge ahead; this is a vast, undulating, grassy spur that rises progressively towards the upper slopes of Seefin, with several intermediate high points in between. Progressing along here you should pass by a fairly well-preserved corner section of a redundant stone wall that is a reassuring, certain landmark in misty weather.

Continue progressing on a NE bearing across expansive, heather-covered slopes followed by tracking over a stretch of flattish ground that is waterlogged and boggy. The first part of this quagmire is usually quite easy to cross, but further on be careful to avoid more difficult ground over on the R, and never place any of your steps on light, green-coloured patches, as these invariably indicate really treacherous ground below! Avoiding such places, climb to the top of the rounded hillock directly ahead, where you will reach the temporary respite of walking across springy, heather-covered slopes. There are also distinctive outcrops of sandstone near the top.

From here, continue NE across the next broad, shallow hause, where you need to cross over a peaty channel to connect with a line of fencing over on your R. From here on, this fence will prove to be a most helpful guide in inclement weather. Be careful, therefore, to turn R ahead, as this fencing does, in order to maintain your important NE bearing and to by-pass another knoll rising to your

L. A boggy dip then has to be crossed, and this will bring you to a stile that provides an easy crossing of another fence running at right angles to your direction of approach.

Following this, some quite ingenious forward planning is required before you decide just how best to get around the series of bog pools and waterlogged ground lying ahead. This is before drier ground is once again reached as you gradually track up on to

Å **12:2** Evening sunlight darting around Lough Caragh

the higher slopes above. Along here, you will come to a larger pool of undrained surface water; it is usually best to contour around this to the L, before being careful to re-establish contact with the faithful wire fence. Then small mounds have to be circumnavigated before the going underfoot above these obstacles becomes less exacting as heathers once more cushion your upward footsteps.

Further on, you have the relative luxury of a narrow track to lead you, this appearing over to the L of, and just above, the wire fence. Then venture more to your L and climb up the rising, stony ground to reach a trig point just above. Continue a short distance further W from here across the expansive slopes to reach the summit area of Seefin, which is marked by a significant pile of stones. You are now standing at 493 m (1615 ft), the highest point of the route, and if your feet are still reasonably dry you will have done very well indeed! Given clear weather, the all-round panoramas from here are simply stunning. Many of the highlights of these have previously been mentioned. However, from here there are extensive new vistas, particularly so northwards of the riveting seascapes that disclose the fascinating features of the strands of Rossbehy and Inch. These pinch together the waters of Dingle Bay, with the high mountains of the Dingle Peninsula, lorded over by the Brandon Massif, rising majestically in the distance beyond.

Be careful to start your adventurous descent to the NNE, traversing down steepish, well-drained slopes that soon become rather slippery as they cross loose, peat-covered ground. Grassy and heather-covered hillsides are reached further down, but here the angle of descent continues to be steeply inclined. Then be vigilant in misty conditions to veer NE, to follow the direction of a heather-clad spur that branches off that way on the R. Several sheep tracks are bisected along the next part of the descent, and lower down trim your approach to head directly towards a number of turf-cutting access tracks that straddle the flatter ground along the spur below.

Turn R along the first track that you reach, to then pass by a small pool off to your R. From here, follow the obvious continuation tracks down towards the valley containing Lough Caragh, progressing further NE and then E across more sheltered slopes. The track swings around to the R and then zigzags further down the hillsides along a gentle slope where the going along a green sward is easy. The upper edge of a strip of conifer trees is then skirted, and near here a side turning on the R that only leads to a farmstead needs to be avoided.

Beyond these features, a hairpin bend to the R marks the northern-most extremity of the route. Then, at the crossroads below, turn R again to commence the final, return legs of the route, initially by progressing southwards along another section of the well-signed Kerry Way. From here, just keep to the elevated, undulating, narrow lane as it winds beneath the formidably steep, eastern slopes of Seefin, these rearing up on your R. About 3½ km (just over 2 miles) further on, you will connect with your outward route at MR 682882 again. Turn L here to retrace your steps, on this occasion downhill, to where you parked your vehicle.

Suitability of Walk and Associated Places of Interest for Families

This adventurous walk over some exposed, wet and rugged ground is not suitable for young children! Older ones, such as teenagers who are strong and hardy and who enjoy a sensible challenge, should relish the walk. However, either take these children there under supervision or ensure that the weather is likely to remain fine during the whole time that they will be crossing the quite demanding, uncharted higher ground.

Places of Interest

KERRY BOG VILLAGE MUSEUM

This popular tourist attraction is located beside the main N70 road, only a short distance from the walk. John and Olive Mulvihill lovingly and authentically created it. John is also the enthusiastic chairman of the associated Kerry Bog Pony Society. The village depicts a number of dwellings and their contents that are exact replicas of those used in Ireland in the early 1800s. Here you will be able to see how Jeremiah Mulvihill (note the surname), a turf cutter, lived; the forge of Jack Bell O'Sullivan; the abode of Phil McGillycuddy, a stable house and dairy; Denny's hen house; the cottage of Denny Riordan, the village labourer; and the home of Paddy Brown, who was a thatcher hailing from the district of Caragh Lake.

There are toilets and a well-stocked gift shop on the site, and excellent refreshment facilities are located adjacent in the form of the Red Fox Inn and Restaurant, where traditional Irish music is featured. Kerry bog ponies may be seen in the nearby fields. These quite small ponies, about 10 or 11 hands high, were formerly used for transporting turf from the bogs (hence their name), but they almost became extinct, and by 1994 there were only 20 such animals left in the whole of Ireland. The aim at the village is to save the bog pony from extinction and, by breeding from them (there are now five breeding mares here), to increase their numbers both in Kerry and further afield. This commendable project has the support of the Irish Genetic Resources Conservation Trust.

Further enquiries about the bog village and the affectionate ponies should be directed to:

John and Olive Mulvihill
Kerry Bog Village Museum
Glenbeigh
Co Kerry
Tel: 066 9769184/9769288

SKELLIG ROCKS (AND SKELLIG HERITAGE CENTRE)

fact/ile

START/FINISH

Leave your vehicle either near Ballinskelligs Pier (MR 433645), in Portmagee (MR 371729), or at the Skellig Heritage Centre on Valencia Island (MR 371734), depending upon from where you sail.

GRADING

Easy/straightforward (providing you do not mind climbing up a lot of steps and you have a head for heights!) (colour-coded BLUE)

WALKING TIME ALLOWANCE

The very short walk from where you disembark and the subsequent climb to the site of the monastery take very little time indeed. However, there is much to see and absorb along the way and when you get there, so pace yourself accordingly in order that you make the very most of your limited time on the island.

DISTANCE

1.2 km (0.7 miles)

TOTAL HEIGHT GAINED

170 m (560 ft)

HIGHEST POINT

Remains of monastery — 170 m (560 ft)

digest o/walk

PARKING

There is adequate parking at or near each of the embarkation points for the small boats that will take you to the Skellig Rocks. However, some of these places are very popular and busy at peak holiday times; so the advice is get there early, and certainly well before your boat is due to sail!

Skellig Rocks
(and Skellig Heritage Centre)

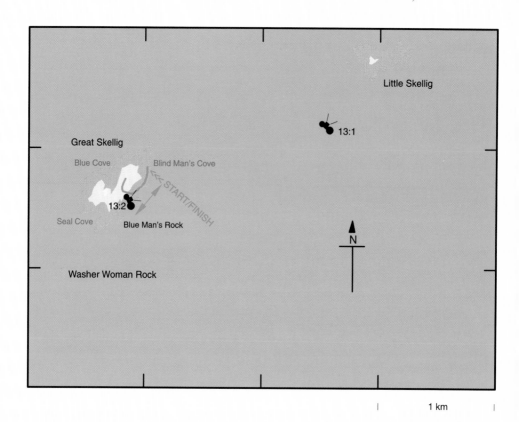

1 km

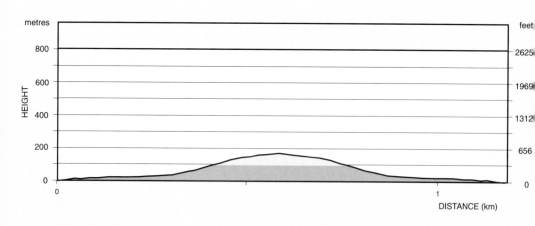

OVERVIEW/INTEREST

- The exploration starts with a bracing sail across the open sea.
- Sail past Little Skellig and disembark on the larger Great Skellig.
- Fantastic rock scenery, with steep cliff faces rearing up from the ocean depths below.
- Chance to climb up to the site of an early Christian monastery, known the world over.
- Extensive colonies of several varieties of sea birds.
- Opportunity to visit the nearby Skellig Heritage Centre.

GRADIENTS

There is one fairly steep and quite demanding climb up a stepped way to reach the beehive huts and oratories of the monastery perched near the top of Great Skellig.

AMENITIES

There are none on the rocks other than those you improvise out of sight of others; so take refreshments with you and drink sparingly before you set out!

MAPS, FOOTPATHS AND WAYSIGNS

OS DISCOVERY SERIES 1:50 000 — NUMBER 83 (KERRY)
An obvious way leads from the jetty to the steps rising steeply to the monastery above. No signs are needed to get there.

GETTING STARTED

All three areas where you may normally wish to park your vehicle are located at the western end of the Iveragh Peninsula, off the main N70 'Ring of Kerry' road. Ballinskelligs is located on the western shores of Ballinskelligs Bay and is reached either by travelling S along the R566 road from the direction of Cahersiveen or by means of the R567 westwards from Waterville. The most convenient way to reach Portmagee is to travel W along the R565 road, and near here you will find the Skellig Heritage Centre located just across the channel, crossed by a road bridge, on nearby Valencia Island. Alternatively, the Skellig Heritage Centre and Portmagee can be accessed by using the short car ferry crossing from Reenard Point to Knight's Town and then travelling SW along Valencia Island.

After jumping off the boat at Blind Man's Cove on Great Skellig just follow the obvious way leading up from the rocky landing stage.

Organisation of Walk and Associated Excursion

This will very much depend upon the timings of the boats, and although there are scheduled sailings, these could be affected by the weather. Assuming reasonably calm conditions, most of the boats depart from either the Portmagee area or Ballinskelligs from about 10 a.m. onwards, returning to the mainland during the early afternoon. These timings appear to suit most visitors. If you possibly can, make a prior booking and try to choose a day when only light winds are forecast to blow.

From the author's personal experiences, the advice is to select a boat that is manned by two crewmen! This is because there is often a swell at the landing stage at Great Skellig, even in relatively calm conditions, and the courageous step off the boat can consequentially be quite tricky, particularly so for those who are not used to striding across a yawning gap. It is therefore essential that the boat is properly secured and, when needed, that there is an experienced and reassuring helping hand to get you safely on to the island. Also, it is strongly advised that any children with you wear a quality life-jacket and that in no circumstances you allow your very young beloved ones to accompany you.

Assuming you set off on a mid-morning sail and have to allow time to get to your embarkation point, you should plan to have a look around the Skellig Heritage Centre when you get back from the rocks.

∦ **13:1** THE POINTED PEAKS OF LITTLE SKELLIG

Alternatively, in order to derive most from the adventurous visit to the rocks, try to arrange a visit to the heritage centre on a day previous to your sailing.

Description of Walk

There is little to tell you that is not obvious when you get there! The exploration obviously starts with a reasonably lengthy sail, the exact duration of which will vary with the speed of your boat and the prevailing weather conditions. For most people, the sea crossing is one of the highlights of the day, and the views, either sailing past craggy Puffin Island or rounding Bolus Head, depending upon where you start from, are simply stunning. No sooner have you finished feasting on these than there is the exciting approach to Skellig Rocks to absorb your attention. These two vast chunks of pointed rock, some 12 km (8 miles) SW of Valencia Island, have been described as standing up like fairytale castles from the swirling Atlantic Ocean. As you approach these fantastic sentinels and recall their fascinating history and archaeology, much more poetic descriptions than this are quite likely to occur to you.

Make your way, unhurriedly, from the landing spot, walking southwards along the wide, surfaced way that threads around the eastern side of the island towards the helicopter pad and the lighthouse, climbing up from the edge of the sea as it does so. When last visited by the author, it was not possible to walk all the way to the end of the roadway, but the place where you need to turn R to climb the steps leading up to the remains of the monastery was readily accessible. This spot is obvious, and the flat rocks and open ground hereabouts provide relatively comfortable perches for you to consume some refreshments and to absorb the special and unique ambience of the place.

The subsequent climb up the wide, stone steps (one of the monks' stairways) overcomes what nature had designed to be inaccessible! The way spirals steeply upwards across the rock faces and in a couple of places there is some limited exposure, so do be careful where you are placing each of your footsteps and, when not passing by people coming down, keep towards the middle of the stone slabs. The views during the ascent are simply stunning and they take in not only the immediate spectacular cliff faces and their feathered inhabitants but nearby Little Skellig and, in favourable visibility, also extensive parts of the rugged coastline of the mainland as well.

Keep going up, realising that in all there are some 2300 steps throughout the island! These link the three landing points, Blue Cove, South Landing and Blind Man's Cove (with which you are now familiar), with the monastic site and the lofty pinnacles above. Fortunately, you do not have to go up all of these today! The remains of the monastery then appear quite suddenly, and as you take time to inspect these at your leisure, you will discover that the principal buildings consist of the well-preserved remains of six corbelled-stone beehive huts and two boat-shaped oratories. The site and thoughts of how the monks survived there in this hostile environment and inaccessible place during the winter months may once again result in your fertile imagination going into overdrive!

When you have seen enough and time is pressing on, simply retrace your steps downward, back towards the landing stage, to arrive there before the embarkation time stipulated previously by your boatman.

▲ **13:2** The adventurous way that clings to the sheer cliff faces at Great Skellig

Suitability of Walk and Associated Places of Interest for Families

As is clear from the description of the walk above, this particular excursion is not suitable for young children. However, many families with teenagers should enjoy a visit to the Skellig Rocks immensely, and apart from the sightseeing, there is a valuable educational aspect to such a trip. The whole family should like wandering around the Skellig Heritage Centre on Valencia Island, with its highly recommended exhibits and extensive facilities.

Places of Interest

SKELLIG HERITAGE CENTRE

This fine, spacious and very popular major visitor centre is located on Valencia Island, just across the water from the village of Portmagee on the mainland. The impressive site was developed by Cork/Kerry Tourism and its theme is 'The Skellig Experience' where the following four aspects of the Skellig Rocks are sensitively exhibited:

- The history and archaeology of Great Skellig's early Christian monastery
- The sea birds (including gannets, guillemots, kittiwakes, puffins, razorbills, shearwaters and storm petrels) that frequent the two rocks, including their habitats and worldwide migrations
- The lighthouses that have aided mariners for over 160 years
- The underwater wonderland surrounding the rocks, considered to be equal in colour and magic to that supported by any other sea worldwide

There is easy access to the buildings for disabled visitors, a theatre where a super audiovisual show, 'The Call of the Skelligs', runs at regular intervals, a gift and craft shop, an attractive refreshment area where light snacks are available, and cloakrooms with dedicated facilities for the disabled and for baby-changing.

The Skellig Heritage Centre has something for all and, for those interested, it is definitely a place not to be missed!

For further details or to arrange a group visit contact:

John O'Sullivan
Manager
Skellig Heritage Centre
Valencia Island
Co Kerry
Tel: 066 9476306
Fax: 066 9476351

It has previously been advocated that you exercise some care in selecting who ships you to the rocks! A list of boat operators that you may choose from, these listed in alphabetical sequence of surname, is provided below:

Brendan Casey, Cahersiveen (Tel: 066 9472437)
Des Lavelle, Valencia Island (Tel: 066 9476124)
Dan McCrohan, Valencia Island (Tel: 066 9476142)
Patrick Murphy, Valencia Island (Tel: 066 9477156)
Seanie Murphy, Valencia Island (Tel: 066 9476214)
Brendan O'Keeffe, Portmagee (Tel: 066 9477103)
Michael O'Sullivan, Waterville (Tel: 066 9474255)
Joe Roddy, Waterville (Tel: 066 9474268)
Dermot Walsh, Valencia Island (Tel: 066 9476120)

V OVERLEAF: THE GREAT BLASKET ISLAND FERRY ABOUT TO REACH THE MAINLAND AT DUNQUIN

DINGLE
PENINSULA
WALKS

Dingle Peninsula Walks

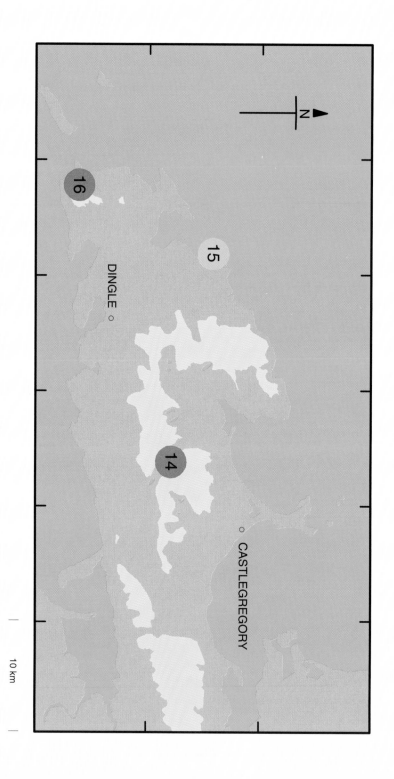

DINGLE PENINSULA

LANDSCAPES AND OPPORTUNITIES FOR SHORT WALKS

The Dingle Peninsula is one of my favourite places, and I suspect many other dedicated walkers share this view. The rugged landscapes towards the western end of the peninsula are dominated by the overpowering majesty of the huge bulk of the Brandon Massif. Brandon Mountain is a firm favourite with many people, and although there is no way you can stand on the top of it by means of a short walk, there are many possibilities of getting to grips with it without too much exertion. One possibility is to climb towards the entrance of the eask (a glaciated staircase containing several paternoster lakes) from Faha. The mountain road over Connor Pass also provides an elevated starting-point from which short walks may be attempted, in several directions, across relatively high and exposed ground.

Contrasting with these high places, much of the coastal margin is suitable for relaxing walking, be this idling along a sandy beach such as at Inch Strand, Ventry Harbour or perhaps around the Fahamore headland, or a more energetic and bracing ramble along the spectacular cliff tops at the likes of Ballydavid Head, near Brandon Point or above Sauce Creek.

The tough Old Red Sandstone and associated strata of which much of the surface rock of the peninsula is composed also present opportunities for getting to the top of hills and mountains that rise to heights between the two extremes mentioned above. It is possible to walk to some of these from only short distances away, and the summit of Mount Eagle at the westerly tip of the peninsula exemplifies one such place.

To summarise, in this land of rugged high mountains, narrow knife-edged ridges, fantastic scooped-out combes, corrie lakes, formidable steep cliff faces, gushing watercourses and tumbling waterfalls, not to mention challenging boggy ground, it is still possible to pick your way with care to a wonderful selection of superb, relatively high vantage points in order to admire the breathtaking scenery surrounding you or, alternatively, to do this from just a few feet above sea level, both of these whilst undertaking short walking expeditions.

Places of Interest Associated with Walking and the Great Outdoors

Once again, the superb topography must take pride of place in terms of places of interest when visiting this peninsula. Apart from walking across this fascinating terrain, two roads, the one that snakes around Slea Head and the one that contorts over Connor Pass, provide opportunities for scenic drives that may be conveniently combined with walking in either area.

There are also delights and fascinations connected with the sea. Boat excursions may be taken from Dingle Harbour, Smerwick Harbour and other places. These include both pleasure cruises and fishing trips, and a ferry sails from Dunquin to Great Blasket Island during the summer months, weather permitting. There is a world-class aquarium located at Dingle town, and from the recently constructed marina in Dingle it is possible to obtain sailing lessons and to arrange diving and snorkelling in some of the finest waters for these activities in Western Europe. Clean, sandy beaches are plentiful, and these range from sweeping strands several miles in length to tiny secluded coves hidden away beneath high cliffs.

The Dingle Peninsula is rich in sites of special archaeological interest and these include Iron Age forts, prehistoric beehive huts, megalithic tombs, the remains of a monastic site and an early Christian prayer cell. There is also a visitor centre near Dunquin dedicated to interpreting the heritage of the nearby Blasket Islands.

Choice of Walks and Associated Places of Interest

With much to choose from, the three short walks selected tend to favour exploring the higher ground. Walk 14, starting from Lough Anscaul, heads northwards to cross the mountainous spine of the peninsula, albeit using a relatively low saddle. Walk 15 is a romp around the cliffs at Ballydavid Head, with the possibility of combining this with also leaving impressions of your bootprints on Great Blasket Island, whilst Walk 16 takes you to the top of Mount Eagle.

Walking Guides, Accommodation and Eating Out

WALKING GUIDES
South West Walks, an organisation based in Tralee that specialises in arranging walking tours, providing guides for daily walks and assisting independent walkers

both in the Dingle Peninsula and elsewhere in Ireland, arranged for one of their expert local guides to accompany us on our more challenging forays into the high mountains of the peninsula. This was Tony O'Callaghan, who is a native of these parts. Tony turned out to be a real charmer and in his knowledgeable company we learned much, observed a great deal and walked in assured safety.

We have also been accompanied by another guide, Michael O'Shea, whose healthy, rugged features and disposition perfectly reflect the name of his outdoor leisure shop which is located in Dingle town and aptly named 'The Mountain Man'.

CONTACT DETAILS

South West Walks Ireland Ltd
40 Ashe Street
Tralee
Co Kerry
Tel: 066 7128733
24-hour: 061 393419
Fax: 066 7128762
Email: swwi@iol.ie

Michael O'Shea
The Mountain Man
Strand Street
Dingle
Co Kerry
Tel: 066 9152390
Fax: 066 9152396
Mobile phone: 087 2550334

ACCOMMODATION

Our normal preference for accommodation is to stay at comfortable and friendly bed and breakfast establishments and to eat out in the evenings at places of choice wherever we then happen to be. True to form, this is what we have done until quite recently whilst touring and walking around the Dingle Peninsula. However, on the last two occasions we travelled there, we broke with our self-imposed convention by staying and enjoying the life of Riley at a really superb premier hotel! This was at the famous Dingle Skellig Hotel, and based on our immensely enjoyable experiences of its leisure facilities, bedrooms, hospitality, service, dining arrangements and delicious food etc., it came as no surprise to learn that this hotel, which positively encourages walkers to stay there, was awarded the prestigious 1998 Hotel of the Year (Ireland) award by Les Routiers. In the low season the hotel offers a selection of bargain breaks, and these are particularly good value should you feel you deserve a few days sampling that extra bit of luxury.

133

ACCOMMODATION REGISTER

Hotel/Guest House	Rooms en suite		Rooms other		Open
Dingle Skellig Hotel Dingle Co Kerry Tel: 066 9151144 Fax: 066 9151501 Email: dsk@iol.ie	115 bedrooms providing the ultimate in luxury				For most of year
Robert Ashe Ashe's Guest House Spa Road Dingle Co Kerry Tel: 066 9151197	F D T S	3 3 0 0	F D T S	0 0 0 0	All year
Bernie Bambury Bambury's Guest House Mail Road Dingle Co Kerry Tel: 066 9151244/9151786	F D T S	8 4 0 0	F D T S	0 0 0 0	All year
Kathleen Dillon Dillon's Connor Pass Road Dingle Co Kerry Tel: 066 9151724	F D T S	1 3 0 0	F D T S	0 0 0 0	All year
Kathleen and P J O'Connor Four Winds Anascaul Co Kerry Tel: 066 9157168 (Also self-catering flats)	F D T S	2 2 0 0	F D T S	0 0 2 0	All year
Kitty Bronson Abhainn Mhór Cloghane Co Kerry Tel: 066 7138211	F D T S	1 1 1 0	F D T S	0 0 0 1	All year

Rooms: F = Family; D = Double; T = Twin; S = Single

EATING OUT

More recently we have dined in style at the Dingle Skellig Hotel. By way of a change from this indulgence we also enjoyed the delicious bar meals served at Máire de Barra's pub at Dingle pierhead (Tel: 066 9151215). On the other side of the peninsula we also found O'Connor's bar and restaurant at Cloghane (Tel: 066 7138113) very much to our liking.

Apart from these, Dingle town bristles with places where you can eat, and these range from elegant restaurants serving gourmet meals in elegant surroundings to pub grub washed down with the black stuff whilst listening to traditional Irish music above the lively din going on there.

LOUGH ANSCAUL AND THE GLENNAHOO VALLEY (AND THE BEACH)

factile

START/FINISH
Start from scenic car park at Lough Anscaul — MR 582052
Finish at junction of path and minor road — MR 547105

GRADING
Moderate/challenging (colour-coded RED)

WALKING TIME ALLOWANCE
3.5 hours

DISTANCE
8.5 km (5.3 miles)

TOTAL HEIGHT GAINED
290 m (950 ft)

HIGHEST POINT
Crest of ridge — 370 m (1215 ft)

digestwalk

PARKING
Remote, scenic car park holds about eight cars. (Note: This is a linear walk and, therefore, ideally two vehicles should be used, one positioned near the end of the walk where, unfortunately, there is only very limited space; obtain permission to park on private ground thereabouts should this prove necessary. Otherwise, arrange transport to collect you from near the end of the route, just after your estimated time of arrival there.)

LOUGH ANSCAUL AND THE
GLENNAHOO VALLEY (AND THE BEACH)

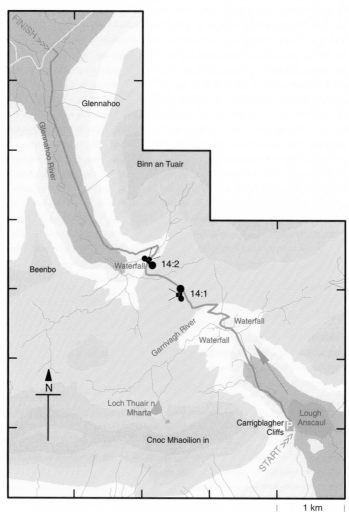

FINISH >>

Glennahoo

Binn an Tuair

Glennahoo River

Waterfall 14:2

Beenbo

14:1

Garrivagh River

Waterfall

Waterfall

N

Loch Thuair n Mharta

Carrigblagher Cliffs

P

Lough Anscaul

Cnoc Mhaoilion in

START >>

1 km

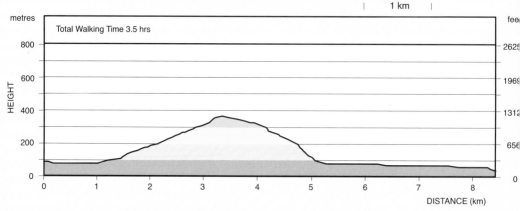

Total Walking Time 3.5 hrs

metres

800

600

HEIGHT

400

200

0

0   1   2   3   4   5   6   7   8

DISTANCE (km)

fee

2625

1969

1312

656

0

OVERVIEW/INTEREST

- Delights of Lough Anscaul, surrounded by spectacular mountain scenery.
- The route climbs past a series of cascading waterfalls.
- Fantastic views from the higher ground whilst crossing over the ridge.
- Adventurous descent into the upper reaches of the Glennahoo Valley.
- Chance to see shepherds and their dogs at work.
- Opportunity to laze about on a nearby beach at either end of the walk.

GRADIENTS

There is a gradual and prolonged climb to reach the higher ground of the main spur that threads E to W along the peninsula. Following a fairly flat crossing of the high ground, there is a steep descent into the upper end of the Glennahoo Valley. The final section of the walk is northwards along the valley, then treading down gently inclined slopes.

AMENITIES

None.

MAPS, FOOTPATHS AND WAYSIGNS

OS DISCOVERY SERIES 1:50 000 — NUMBER 70 (KERRY)

The walk commences along a mountain road, the surface of which progressively deteriorates into a rough, stony track towards the top of the pass. A fairly flat plateau then has to be crossed where the way is quite obscure in places before better defined, narrow paths are located towards the far side. These lead down into the valley beyond and, similar to the way up, they upgrade into wide tracks and then narrow lanes as you descend further along the valley.

There are some boggy patches during the ascent and the flattish ground along the top of the spur is often waterlogged after wet weather.

The route is quite poorly signed with only spasmodic waysigns, but these are being improved due to the efforts of local organisations interested in opening the area up for enjoyable walking.

GETTING STARTED

Lough Anscaul is located just over 3 km (nearly 2 miles) to the NNW of the village of Anascaul. Turn N off the main N86 road at the village and follow the minor roads northwards through several tiny hamlets to reach the lough. A gate needs to be opened but there is a surfaced, if potholed, road leading all the way to the parking area above the lough.

Start the walk by directing your footsteps further northwards along the valley, using the extension of the public road to do this.

The crossing of the high ground and the subsequent important location of the recommended safest way down can become a real challenge should mist descend. Therefore, unless you are proficient in navigating in these exacting conditions, do not attempt the crossing, opting instead to return to Lough Anscaul along the familiar approach paths and tracks that you used on the way up.

ORGANISATION OF WALK AND ASSOCIATED EXCURSION

A quite leisurely crossing of this high ground from Lough Anscaul to the northern coast of the peninsula can be completed within half a day. This will leave plenty of time to laze around on one of the splendid beaches located near either end of the walk, and also to recover one of your vehicles, should this be required. The suggestion is that you complete the walk in the morning, leaving the rest of the day for the beach or whatever else you choose to do — perhaps even walking back!

DESCRIPTION OF WALK

The surrounds of Lough Anscaul are both pretty and awesome. These remote, tranquil waters are trapped within a scooped-out basin that is surrounded by steeply rising craggy peaks that completely encapsulate the lough, save for the narrow entrance through which you arrived at this sublime spot. On sunny mornings when the air is still, the mountains are reflected to perfection on the glassy surface waters of the lough, and in these conditions it may take some effort to get those walkers with cameras away from here!

When you do, you will immediately be walking beneath steep, rocky ground and boulder fields that sweep up to your L. These form the lower slopes of Cnoc Mhaoilionáin, the summit of which remains out of view. The northern end of the lough is soon left behind, as is a metal gate that you have to pass through. Continue northwards up this spectacular, glaciated valley, threading your way along the winding track between imposing crags that then start to enclose the glen on both sides. The way continues along a fairly flat section beside a meandering stream on an excellent track for walking, and you pass through more gates and then between redundant stone pillars.

Following this, the route starts to rise, moderately to begin with but this steepens further on as the surface of the track changes from compacted earth and stones to grass. When you reach another gate above, pause and turn around to absorb the splendid views from this position back down along the valley. Beyond this, you traverse along a grassy ledge, high above a steepish drop down to the Garrivagh River below. The main stream is fed by several tributary watercourses that cascade down the steep sides of the valley, cutting ever-deepening V-nicks into the green hillsides as they do so.

Your way bends around to the L, tracking NW above a series of more impressive waterfalls that plunge down a narrow gully over exposed, layered rocks. The ascent now becomes rougher as you have to weave a way across boulders and loose stones, following a narrow path that curves further L up the rising valley. Higher up, the Garrivagh River is bridged by a concrete structure to your R, and tributary streams feeding into the main river then have to be crossed several more times as the continuation way zigzags up steeper slopes lining the upper reaches of the valley system.

A series of long traverses, with acute bends at their ends, will lead you towards the higher ground of the broad ridge above. It can become quite boggy along here and usually some evasive action is called for. Incremental height continues to be gained up comfortably inclined gradients along a section of the way that is obvious. Then it becomes a bit different! Near to the top of the slopes, be careful to ignore the first stony side path that leads off, more steeply on the R, in order not to

14:1 CROSSING THE HIGH GROUND THAT CONNECTS SLIEVENAGOWER AND BEENOSKEE

add to the considerable erosion hereabouts. However, a short distance further on, do veer R at an inviting spot across the open terrain to then head further up the rough, grassy slopes on a WSW bearing, veering NW.

A short section of soggy, wet ground has to be crossed before you will locate another clearly identified broad track that leads over higher ground along a northward diagonal. This way then bends L to reach the apex of the ridge, where the surrounding ground is often submerged under lying water. This spongy surface should be crossed on a predominately NW bearing. Then manoeuvre slightly to the R to follow a shallow, stony channel for a short distance before climbing out of it back on to the open, grassy slopes. These then lead marginally downhill, tracking NNW.

A short distance further on, you should locate an indistinct sheep track going your way, and this will provide a useful aid to crossing further sweeping stretches of quite often soggy grasslands. Do watch out for nasty holes in the ground along here! The compensation for your considerable route-finding efforts in this particular vicinity are that in fine weather you will be able to absorb the most spectacular mountain scenery from this elevated position. To the west, the craggy ridge rises, undulating as it does so, towards the fascinating, high terrain of Slievenalecka, Slievanea and An Cnapán Mór, whilst in the opposite direction towards NE the compelling views are towards the more rounded summit area of Beenoskee.

Track on, but when you reach a shallow depression ahead, be careful to bear L, thereby changing your heading towards WNW for a short distance. Continue to veer L to then enter a grassy channel, down which a small watercourse flows. For the time being track along the L-hand bank of the stream, progressing NW to reach and then follow a distinct stony track as it curves to the L, heading further downhill along the course of the stream. Then cross the streamlet at some inviting spot, after which you should be extremely careful to head due N in order to avoid the steep cliffs that now begin to plunge down on your L!

Within a very short distance you must be vigilant to connect with a clearly defined, grassy path that immediately tracks around to the R, leading you across steeply falling slopes. In clear weather, the most magnificent views open up from here, these down into the upper reaches of the glaciated valley hundreds of feet

below, being perpetually deepened by several tributaries of the Glennahoo River flowing swiftly down into it. The continuation path then traverses very steeply across a side valley, and this section involves the adventurous crossing of a cascading mountain stream, the confines of which are rounded to your L by means of an acute U-turn. The views to be observed on the way down along here are simply fantastic, with the high peaks of the Brandon Massif to the

14:2 DESCENDING TOWARDS THE HEAD OF THE GLENNAHOO VALLEY

NW providing the most spectacular backcloth. However, when admiring these, always do this from a secure position, being ever mindful of the exceptionally steep, grassy fall-aways on your L! The lengthy downward incline continues on the far side of the stream heading WSW where you pass by a waysign that indicates the route of a local walk; it reads 'Siúlóid Gleann — na hUamha — (Binn a' Tuair)'. More waterfalls now appear, these cascading down clefts in the near-vertical cliff faces on your L that you have skilfully avoided! The prolonged descent continues as you veer around to the R and then zigzag back L to drop down towards the floor of the valley, passing above a cluster of long-abandoned stone buildings.

Another marker post is positioned at the bottom of the slopes, and from here continue NW veering NNW along the steep, U-shaped valley of the Glennahoo River that is now hemmed in by the steep slopes of the craggy Beenbo ridge to the W and the more rounded contours of Binn an Tuair to the E. Keep along the obvious path and this will lead you past sheep pens positioned further down the valley. Beyond this, a wide cart track becomes established and you then need to pass through a rickety gateway followed by opening a metal gate further on. Then ignore the first turning followed by a path, both leading off to the L, to then turn L to cover the remaining short distance down to the road below. Either walk on from here to recover your parked vehicle or wait, if you have to, to be collected by your prearranged transport.

SUITABILITY OF WALK AND ASSOCIATED PLACES OF INTEREST FOR FAMILIES

The full walk, with its climbing, the rough terrain at the top of the ridge and the steep, exacting descent, is considered far too difficult for most children, other than strong, hardy teenagers who are experienced at being out amongst the mountains following a route that is not always obvious. Families with younger children are advised to venture up the valley as far as the first waterfalls, and after resting there, to turn back when they consider that their offspring have had enough.

PLACES OF INTEREST

NEARBY BEACHES

Excellent, clean, sandy beaches are to be discovered fairly close to both ends of the walk. To the N the sweeping sands of Brandon Bay may be conveniently accessed at Fermoyle where a car park has been thoughtfully positioned, whilst to the SE of the village of Anascaul the considerable delights of Inch Strand present an invitation not to be lightly spurned. Here, there are more vast sands, with dunes sheltering these, to lure you towards the distant point of the strand. Parking facilities, toilets, a gift shop and a café also contribute to the overall attraction of this place for holidaymakers.

BALLYDAVID HEAD
(AND THE BLASKET ISLANDS)

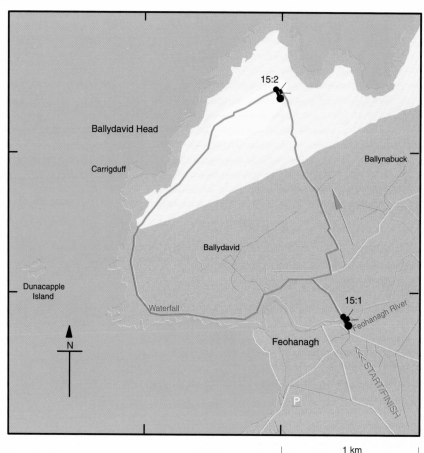

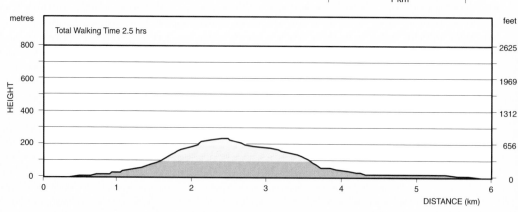

BALLYDAVID HEAD
(AND THE BLASKET ISLANDS)

fact file

START/FINISH
Park near An Cúinne public house —
MR 395097

GRADING
Easy/straightforward (colour-coded
BLUE)

WALKING TIME ALLOWANCE
2.5 hours

DISTANCE
6.0 km (3.7 miles)

TOTAL HEIGHT GAINED
240 m (785 ft)

HIGHEST POINT
Martello tower on Ballydavid Head —
247 m (810 ft)

digest of walk

PARKING
Limited parking with space for about six cars along the verges at the road
junction near An Cúinne public house; if congested there, seek permission to
park at the pub.

OVERVIEW/INTEREST
- Spectacular coastal scenery with high cliffs plunging into the seas far below.
- Revealing views of the westerly aspects of the Brandon Massif.
- Visit to the remains of a Martello lookout tower.
- Section along a sheltered bay.
- Opportunity to visit nearby Smerwick Harbour and the Blasket Islands.

There is a gradual climb to reach the spectacular cliffs of Ballydavid Head. From here it is downhill all the way with a variety of gradients ranging between moderate and almost imperceptible.

None, apart from the pub across the road at the start.

OS DISCOVERY SERIES 1:50 000 — NUMBER 70 (KERRY)

The route is clearly defined for virtually all of the way. It makes use of a succession of minor roads, wide tracks and narrow paths. There is the occasional short linking section across grassy slopes where the correct route is only faintly visible before another certain path is reached.

Apart from along the sections of road used, there are no signs. However, despite this, route finding very rarely presents any significant problems.

Use the exceptionally well-signed Slea Head Scenic Drive circuit to reach the coast near Feohanagh where the suggested parking place for the walk is located.

Head off up the lane leading northwards towards Ballydavid and Ballynabuck, almost immediately crossing over the Feohanagh River.

ORGANISATION OF WALK AND ASSOCIATED EXCURSION

This walk can be completed well within half a day and, therefore, it can be fitted in at almost any time you happen to be in the area. Should you decide to combine the walk with a ferry trip to Great Blasket Island, it will be sensible for you either to start the walk quite early in the morning or, during the longer days of summer, to save this delight for the early evening.

DESCRIPTION OF WALK

The river crossing affords you superb views upstream towards the spectacular heights of the Brandon Massif dominating the eastern skyline in clear weather. The craggy, rocky profiles directly ahead are part of Ballydavid Head promontory, whilst over to your L in good visibility the pointed shapes of the aptly named The Three Sisters headland rise spectacularly out of the ocean depths to the W.

The narrow road rises as it bends sharply to the R, and here the side turning off to the L that you now avoid forms part of your return route. After this, be careful to select a narrow track leading off on the L and this will provide passage between a house and a bungalow. It then tracks moderately uphill leading you further N towards the craggy horizon, high above. On the way there, the track bends to the R and then kinks back to the L as it threads between more dwellings. From this elevated position, given clear visibility, you should obtain some revealing views of the massive bay of Smerwick Harbour to the SW.

The hedged way continues to gain height up the fairly gently sloping hillsides as you pass by prolific crops of blackberries, ripe for picking in the autumn, and, higher up, fuchsias in bloom during the summer months. Soon you will be able to locate Ballydavid Tower amongst the rock features above on your L. This round lookout tower is one of the many Martello towers which, copying the design of towers used as gun fortifications in the Mediterranean, were built around the Irish coastline at the beginning of the nineteenth century.

Having spurned a side turning on the R, pass through two metal gates ahead, the second of which is ingeniously fastened! The wide approach path terminates

人 **15:1** A RIVER CROSSING PROVIDES SUPERB VIEWS UPSTREAM TOWARDS THE BRANDON MASSIF

here at a spot where, if you turn about, you should be rewarded with the most superb, panoramic views across the wide, sweeping valley below. This is attractively dotted with small hamlets, farms and pastures, these all sheltered by the vast, protective slopes of the magnificent Brandon range that rears up steeply to over 3000 ft in the background.

Now, continue to head NNW up the steeper, more rugged terrain heading for the horizon above to the R of the tower. The traverse up these slopes is over firm and well-drained ground and, even better, a faint path becomes established higher up. Keep heading up constrained by a N to NNW bearing to reach the top of the cliff faces at a broad hause between higher ground and to the R of, and still below,

the tower. Walk towards the edge, where from a secure position you may absorb the splendour of steep, almost vertical cliffs plunging hundreds of feet into the swirling white waters of the ocean far below.

When you have seen enough, turn L and begin to climb up the rocky ground that rises above, quickly changing your heading towards SW. Along here, always keep well away from the unstable edges of the continuing steep, dangerous cliff faces on your R. Also, do maintain a constant, firm grip of the wrists of any younger children in your protective care! This final part of the ascent towards the tower will lead you past some interesting, weathered rock formations that resemble a set of giant's teeth. Beyond these jagged protrusions, grassy sheep tracks will lead you across the short remaining distance to the Martello tower, where more fantastic cliff-top views may be observed.

⋀ **15:2** THE FEARSOME COASTLINE BETWEEN BALLYDAVID HEAD AND BRANDON CREEK

When you get there, you will discover that a dilapidated stone wall surrounds the tower, and in this vicinity you may also spot an arctic hare which, as the name suggests, loves the infrequent snowfalls hereabouts. Start your descent by continuing along the ridge, progressing further W veering SW. A firm, grassy way allows you to do this as it threads a path through numerous rocky outcrops, before veering L, away from the cliff faces. More faint tracks will assist your correct route finding across the sloping hillsides and further down you should pass by a short length of dilapidated stone walling.

Leave the protection of the walling to locate and follow another track that will lead you further downhill on your established SW bearing, once again close to more spectacular cliffs over to your R. Further sections of walling are then encountered before the gradient down steepens quite appreciably as your route once more threads between rocks and boulders. Then follow a lengthier section of walling down further, at first keeping to the R of this, before crossing through a convenient gap in it.

You will then reach flatter ground below, which you cross heading S still walking close to the pounding waves. Further on, bear progressively to the L following the edge of the promontory, before heading inland along the coastline and following another faint path that will take you E. A wire fence then has to be crossed but stepping slabs have been placed here to help you over. From here, a better established way leads round and above the sandy bay ahead on your R to then connect with a surfaced lane. Turn R along this to progress further E, where you will connect with another surfaced lane a short distance on. Turn R here to complete the final short section downhill to where you parked your vehicle.

SUITABILITY OF WALK AND ASSOCIATED PLACES OF INTEREST FOR FAMILIES

Apart from the exposure along the cliffs, the walk is suitable for most children except the very young. If you are uncertain do not take your children the whole way round but instead divide the family up, the escorted smaller ones making directly for the sandy beach and, if they are up to it, then climbing some distance up the slopes to rendezvous with the rest of the family during their prolonged descent.

PLACES OF INTEREST

BLASKET ISLANDS

Location and Configuration

The Blasket Islands are located just to the W of the main Slea Head projection, and the nearest point of the largest island, Great Blasket, lies across Blasket Sound about 2 km (1¼ miles) from the mainland at Dunmore Head. There are seven principal islands and these, together with many rocks, are known collectively as The Blaskets. Great Blasket Island is about 6 km (4 miles) long and at its widest point about a kilometre across. Its highest point, Croaghmore, rises to 292 m (960 ft) towards the SW of the island. To the NE of this, the island's second highest point, Slievedonagh, rises to 281 m (920 ft), and near here there is the site of an Iron Age hill fort dating back over 2000 years. Great Blasket Island also had a much more modern village settlement at its NE end, but the inhabitants were moved to the mainland in the early 1950s.

Blasket Centre

The Blasket Centre is situated on the mainland near to the scattered settlement of Dunquin. The centre is signposted from the Slea Head Scenic Drive. The physical appearance of the building has become quite controversial; however, it is inside that matters, and here the story of the Blasket Islands and their colourful history and important contribution to Irish culture are disclosed in a most interesting and spectacular way. Refreshment facilities are also located at the centre.

For further information and guided tours contact:

Booking Office
Blasket Centre
Dunquin
Co Kerry
Tel: 066 9156444
Fax: 066 9156446

Blasket Island Ferry

Weather permitting, during the period from April to October there is a ferry service from Dunquin to Great Blasket Island and this provides opportunities for adventurous walking on the island and visiting important archeological sites located there. (It is advisable to check times of sailings with the harbour authorities or the tourist office in Dingle, the Blasket Centre or through the proprietors of your accommodation.)

MOUNT EAGLE (AND OCEANWORLD AQUARIUM)

fact ile

START/FINISH	DISTANCE
Park at Kildurrihy — MR 353002	7.6 km (4.7 miles)

GRADING	TOTAL HEIGHT GAINED
Moderate/challenging (colour-coded RED)	510 m (1675 ft)

	HIGHEST POINT
	Mount Eagle — 516 m (1695 ft)

WALKING TIME ALLOWANCE	
3.5 hours	

digest walk

PARKING

Limited parking along verges in the tiny hamlet of Kildurrihy. Park considerately and check with local residents that your parked vehicle will not cause them any inconvenience.

OVERVIEW/INTEREST

- The route passes by a sheltered corrie lough.
- Magnificent coastal landscapes, including sightings of the Blasket Islands.
- Superb perspectives of the ranging, westerly slopes of the Brandon Massif.
- Turf-cutting areas are visited.
- Adventurous descent down steep cliff faces.

Mount Eagle
(and Oceanworld Aquarium)

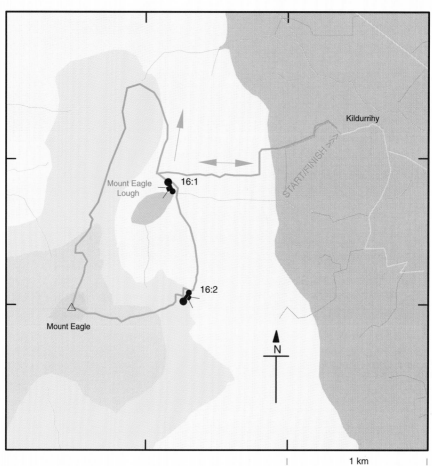

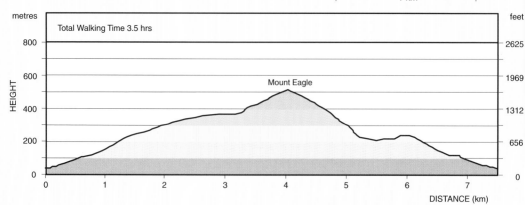

GRADIENTS

There is a gradual, prolonged climb from the starting-point all the way to the summit of Mount Eagle, with some steepish sections along the way. The descent starts quite gently, but further on there is a zigzag traverse down a steep, grassy hillside flanked by rocky outcrops and cliffs. The final section of the way down retraces your outward steps up.

AMENITIES

None.

MAPS, FOOTPATHS AND WAYSIGNS

OS DISCOVERY SERIES 1:50 000 — NUMBER 70 (KERRY)

The ascent is firstly along minor roads. Further up, these degrade into wide and then narrow tracks and paths, but the continuation way is, nearly always, fairly well defined. The route down is across rough, challenging terrain with only limited sections of paths and tracks to guide you until you reach Mount Eagle Lough again. From there you will have no further difficulty in locating your parked vehicle in the hamlet below.

There are a few wet patches on the way up, and more extensive boggy ground has to be crossed during the upper part of the descent.

There are no waysigns along the route.

GETTING STARTED

Assuming your approach is from the Dingle area, use the R559 road (Slea Head Scenic Drive) to motor westwards around Ventry Harbour. Turn R when you reach the crossroads located at MR 370999 and then take the next turning on the L to follow the back roads into the tiny hamlet of Kildurrihy.

Walk uphill out of the hamlet heading westwards towards the higher ground rising ahead.

CAUTIONARY NOTE

When last visited, the paths shown on the OS map to the E of the summit of Mount Eagle did not always coincide with those on the ground! A local walking guide has confirmed this contention.

Should the weather be misty or should a gale be blowing when you reach the top of Mount Eagle, then, unless you are strong, experienced walkers and are well versed in navigational skills, you are strongly advised, for reasons of safety, to descend along the well-defined approach route that you used to reach this point.

Organisation of Walk and Associated Excursion

The full walk will take a good half-day and it may conveniently be combined with either a drive around Slea Head or a visit to Dingle town. The exceptional Oceanworld Aquarium is located in the town, and if you decide to visit this attraction allow yourselves a couple of hours, for, in addition to the fish swimming about, there are spacious refreshment facilities and much more to digest there.

Description of Walk

Fork L ahead to continue gaining height along a rougher, surfaced lane that rises more steeply. Then, bypass a side turning on the L, opting to keep straight ahead, heading directly towards the communications pylon now in view above. As you head towards this mast, the most splendid panoramas open up behind you when the weather is clear. These include both the westerly slopes of the Brandon Massif and the contrasting, low-lying features of Ventry and Dingle harbours, the twin highlights of a riveting coastline. When visibility is exceptionally good, the pointed peaks of the MacGillycuddy's Reeks, the highest mountains in all of Ireland, provide a fascinating, distant horizon.

The obvious continuation way passes close by the pylon before the surfaced track terminates quite abruptly at a metal gate. Pass through the gate and make your way down to the shores of Mount Eagle Lough. This sheltered spot is ideal for taking some deserved refreshments as you relax for a spell beside the gently lapping waves of these secluded, trapped waters. If you happen to have young children with you, getting here could even represent the achievement of your main objective for the day. The views across the lough are terrific, with steep, dark cliff faces rising in a series of craggy pitches towards the summit slopes of Mount Eagle, still some considerable height above.

16:1 The refreshing waters of Mount Eagle Lough

To get started again, return to the clearly defined continuation route above. This is an overgrown cart track that traverses up steeper and rougher slopes, which, unfortunately, do contain some waterlogged patches. The way leads N before curving around to the L in the shape of a gigantic horseshoe. More superb views may be absorbed along here when the weather is kind, and the new vistas include the first exposure of the fascinating topography surrounding Smerwick Harbour and Ballydavid Head, both further to the N.

Your way then connects with a better defined, surfaced track. Veer L along this to head southwards, continuing to gain incremental height. In clear weather you should now be able to spot the sprawling summit area of Mount Eagle ahead and also have the thrill of sighting the Basket Islands, a short distance out to sea down on your R. Following a fairly flat section that provides a temporary respite, the track rises considerably more steeply as it winds up towards the top of the huge mountain.

Further up, the stony track, which is in fact a turf-cutting access road, abruptly terminates at an area littered with partly harvested peat, left there to dry out. At this point, continue walking S traversing across rising heathland to reach the summit of Mount Eagle along any of several final approach paths. A trigonometrical point is positioned on the vast, flat-topped summit area at a height of 516 m (1695 ft). In favourable weather conditions and when you are not being buffeted about by strong winds, spend some time exploring these extensive slopes in order to take in the many splendid views, some of which are unfortunately obscured from the very top by the rounded contours just below. You should by now be familiar with most of these and the highlights should be little more than a test of your memory.

As stated earlier, you are strongly advised to descend from this peak by retracing your outward steps if it is misty or very windy up there. Otherwise, proceed down the more adventurous descent route towards E. Commence this by heading off ESE from the trig point, initially walking across gentle, expansive, grassy slopes in line with the distant peninsula far below. These slopes gradually steepen, and as they do so, change your direction of descent slightly to the L and towards due E. Then be extremely cautious to skirt above the dangerous cliff faces more to the L still. However, you do need to make contact with this edge, from a safe distance away, to confirm your correct positioning, and this is particularly important when visibility is poor! When you spot this unstable ground, track back towards ESE when necessary, to follow the shape of the steep fall-aways.

During this part of the descent you will have to put up with traversing across some soft, squelchy patches as you continue to surrender height across rough, bumpy ground that is partly covered with long, tufted grasses. The ground ahead then begins to fall appreciably more steeply, and here it is very important that you quickly locate and then follow a well-defined, grassy track that zigzags down the steep slopes in a series of traverses. By doing this you will avoid far more difficult, rocky ground to both L and R!

Keep heading down towards the distant, flat landscapes below. These, in the format of a huge patchwork quilt, disclose an intricate latticework of tiny hamlets and isolated farms that are surrounded by enclosed, sheltered pasturelands continuously being eaten away by flocks of roaming sheep. Further down, this obvious part of the way crosses a huge, grassy bowl scooped out of the otherwise rocky terrain of the steep, rugged hillside. More zigzags follow, these leading you further down across broader, more spacious slopes, where further on a number of stone enclosures, probably used for drying out peat, will be passed.

Beyond these certain, man-made features, the continuation way down, somewhat surprisingly (and perhaps disturbingly), becomes quite obscure and the route forward is then far from obvious. This is particularly so in misty conditions! You now have a choice. The most certain way from here is to continue to head down eastwards until you eventually reach a wall and a wire fence below and over which there is no crossing in this vicinity. If you do this, then turn L to track across rough ground, heading northwards towards the communications aerial that should now, once more, be visible, and always keep close to the walling on your R as you do so. Follow this walling as it turns uphill without ever attempting to cross it. This will lead you towards the eastern tip of Mount Eagle Lough, and further on, you will need to veer L to cross a small section of rough ground, climbing uphill NW to reach the trapped waters of the lough. Obviously, this suggested approach to the lough does involve some climbing back up, because the walling is positioned slightly below this feature. Confident navigators may avoid this by veering L higher up just after they have decended beyond the craggier, rocky spur to their L. They may then traverse downhill across rough, rocky terrain on a northward bearing to reach the shores of Mount Eagle Lough without ever descending significantly below these. The choice here is up to you!

At most water levels in the lough, it is possible to cross over the exit stream with a little agility and ingenuity without getting your feet wet. You do need to achieve this manoeuvre in order to reach the sanctity of the benign, grassy slopes, where perhaps earlier in the day you had some refreshments on the way up. Should torrents of water be flowing out of the lough, either take your boots and socks off before doing a spot of paddling, or carefully cross the stone walling twice just below the mouth of the lough.

From here, all your troubles (if any) are behind you! Simply pass through the metal gate above and then retrace your outward steps back to where you parked your vehicle.

SUITABILITY OF WALK AND ASSOCIATED PLACES OF INTEREST FOR FAMILIES

Mainly due to a combination of the prolonged climbing to reach the summit, the rough, steep ground on part of the way down and some navigational challenges, the full walk as described is not considered suitable for children other than strong, hardy teenagers who might even lend a hand with the route finding. Families with young children should be able to get as far as the lough and enjoy themselves there. They may also venture up the slopes beyond these waters, turning back when they feel they have had enough, which could conceivably be even from the very top of the mountain.

16:2 DESCENDING FROM THE SUMMIT OF MOUNT EAGLE IN THE DIRECTION OF VENTRY HARBOUR WITH LOCAL GUIDE TONY O'CALLAGHAN

PLACES OF INTEREST

OCEANWORLD AQUARIUM

One of the premier visitor attractions of Dingle is the Oceanworld Aquarium, which is sited on the outskirts of the town near to the new marina. This fascinating collection of fish tanks is considered to be amongst the top 10 such venues in the whole of Europe. Here you may walk through an underground tunnel and come face to face with monsters of the deep, including feared sharks. The aquarium attracts over 100,000 visitors each year and with its strong emphasise on protecting and preserving the natural environment — for example over 90 per cent of the fish and other sea creatures on display are recovered from fishing catches, and damaged fish are nurtured back to health before being returned to the sea — the project has much to commend it.

An innovative attraction of the aquarium that goes down particularly well with children of most ages is the 'touch tank'. Here, you can literally gain hands-on experience by being allowed to tickle the fish with your tickling fingers dipped beneath the surface of the water. The fish appear to appreciate this as well! Toilets and spacious refreshment facilities are also available.

For further information or to arrange an escorted group tour contact:

Dingle Oceanworld Aquarium
Dingle, Co Kerry
Tel: 066 9152111; Fax: 066 9152155; Email: marabeo@iol.ie

OVERLEAF: EVENTIDE AT LOUGH INAGH, WITH THE MWEELREA MOUNTAINS FORMING THE DISTANT BACKGROUND

Connemara
and Mayo
Walks

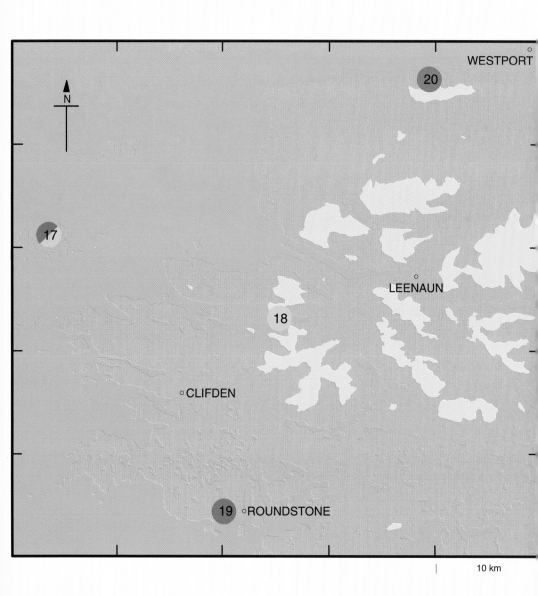

CONNEMARA AND MAYO

LANDSCAPES AND OPPORTUNITIES FOR SHORT WALKS

From a walker's perspective, only superlatives can attempt to describe the magnificent mountainous scenery that occupies the greater area of rugged Connemara and also parts of Mayo. This intricate latticework of disparate, high mountain groupings, formed of mostly Precambrian quartzite rock, is nearly 600 million years old. Long, glaciated, U-shaped valleys, including flooded Killary Harbour, have since wriggled into and divided the high ground, and it is along these and across some of the more modest hills located towards the fringes of the region that visitors wishing to complete short walks must set their sights. Some of the offshore islands, particularly Inishbofin, are also very appropriate for undemanding explorations completed on foot.

Even from these lower altitudes, given fine weather, walkers will be able to marvel at the pointed, quartzite peaks poking up all around them. Perhaps somewhat surprisingly, quite often such viewing positions are amongst the very best, for example the separate summit of Tully Mountain near the coast, which provides superb perspectives right into much of the hinterland of Connemara, including the awesome Twelve Bens. Loughs of all shapes and sizes manage to squeeze into almost every view and these contribute significantly to the pleasing effect of the overall tapestry.

Go and walk in Connemara just once in fine weather and you will, almost inevitably, become yet another enthusiast telling others of its outstanding natural beauty.

PLACES OF INTEREST ASSOCIATED WITH WALKING AND THE GREAT OUTDOORS

Kylemore Abbey, located to the W of Kylemore Lough, and its various seductive features is one of Ireland's major tourist attractions and is well worth a visit. The splendid Westport House and the attractive seaside village of Roundstone offer further contrasting delights to visitors to this wonderfully varied part of Ireland.

Not surprisingly, the fascinations of the sea loom large in these parts. A delight for most children will be a prolonged visit to the 'Ocean's Alive' marine centre, which is located just E of the 'Quay' on the N side of Ballynakill Harbour

(Tel: 095 43473), this perhaps being combined with a boat trip out into the sheltered reaches of the harbour. If you happen to be keen on ploughing through bigger waves, a longer and more adventurous sail is across to Inishbofin.

The more religious-minded walkers, apart from *not* taking their boots off to get to the summit of Croagh Patrick, may also enjoy exploring the Holy Well, reflecting on the 14 Stations of the Cross and wincing at the sharpness of the rocks lining the cave where it is purported St Patrick lay down to sleep at Maumeen in the Maumturk Mountains. You will have to walk there though!

CHOICE OF WALKS AND ASSOCIATED PLACES OF INTEREST

Walk 17 will take you across the water from Cleggan to explore the delights of the tranquil atmosphere and easy pace of life on Inishbofin. Walk 18 combines a sojourn around the grounds of Kylemore Abbey with a more challenging climb to inspect the statue placed part way up the hillside rising steeply above. Walk 19 will take you to the southwestern reaches of Connemara, where you will scale the rugged Errisbeg. Walk 20, your final escapade, will take you to the summit of holy Croagh Patrick and provide a suitable ending to this collection of short walks. At this point you may indulge in some private meditation and perhaps think back over the joyous times that you spent completing the other 19 routes!

WALKING GUIDES, ACCOMMODATION AND EATING OUT

WALKING GUIDES

Christopher Stacey, the walking guide of Wicklow fame, came over and led me on a merry way over much of the challenging, high terrain of Connemara. He also helped me sort out a few of the details on the short walks eventually selected for this book. Contact details, should you wish to get in touch with Christopher, are provided on page 15.

I also had the pleasure of a brief walking interlude with a local expert, Gerry Greensmyth, who operates inclusive walking tours and other guided walking activities from his base at Belclare near Westport. This accompaniment was on the rough scree slopes of Croagh Patrick, where Gerry showed me an escape route that minimised the danger of walkers above you showering loose rock debris down upon you.

CONTACT DETAILS
Gerry Greensmyth
Croagh Patrick Walking Holidays
Belclare View
Belclare
Westport
Co Mayo
Tel/Fax: 098 26090

ACCOMMODATION

Our base camp whenever we have stayed in Connemara has been at the superbly situated Pass Inn and Restaurant near Kylemore. If ever a place was deliberately located in surroundings that, without fail, will seduce you to put your boots on and commence walking in any direction, this without doubt must be it! When you get up each morning and look around you, weather permitting, you will immediately be thrilled with fantastic mountain scenery as fine as any I have observed from any other overnight stop. After a hearty breakfast, as you walk or motor towards these mountains it just gets better and better. At the other end of the day, when you return to your 'room at the inn', you need not venture out again, for there you have the choice of eating in an excellent restaurant or devouring with a flow of liquid a bar meal. Here, you can agreeably fraternise with the congenial locals, one of whom is a highly accomplished musician.

We have also stayed with the Greensmyths at their comfortable guest house in Belclare. Gerry and Bernie will take great care of your needs here; as she supports Gerry's walking business, Bernie knows exactly what walkers want foodwise, and she will also look after your other needs, such as drying wet clothing, exceptionally well too.

Another haven, particularly for family walkers and other family groups, are the luxury holiday apartments recently developed at The Harbour Mill, Westport. Activity holidays, including hillwalking, feature at this splendid centre where you may enjoy the freedom of self-catering.

ACCOMMODATION REGISTER

Hotel/Guest House	Rooms en suite		Rooms other		Open
Rose Rima The Pass Inn and Restaurant Kylemore Connemara Co Galway Tel: 095 41141	F D T S	3 3 5 0	F D T S	0 0 0 0	All year
Gerry and Bernie Greensmyth Belclare View Belclare Westport Co Mayo Tel/Fax: 098 26090	F D T S	3 0 1 0	F D T S	2 0 0 0	April to Oct
Eldon's Hotel Roundstone Connemara Co Galway Tel: 095 35933	F D T S	3 7 9 0	F D T S	0 0 0 0	March to Nov
The Harbour Mill Westport Harbour Westport Co Mayo Tel: 098 28555	● Luxury holiday apartments ● Sleep 3 to 6				

Rooms: F = Family; D = Double; T = Twin; S = Single

EATING OUT

Whilst in Connemara we tend to eat at The Pass Inn, alternating between the restaurant and the downstairs snug bar in a ratio of about 1 : 2. Otherwise, both Clifden and Westport contain a wide range of eating places yet to be tried by us. However, if you happen to be near to Westport in ravenous mode, do give 'The Sheebeen', situated on the coast road near to Belclare, a try. The huge, fresh cod and plateful of chips served here will certainly absorb great volumes of the liquid accompaniment you choose to wash down this delicious food.

INISHBOFIN

fact/ile

START/FINISH

Pier, Bofin Harbour, Inishbofin — MR 537648

GRADING

Easy/straightforward to moderate/ challenging, depending upon weather (colour-coded BLUE/RED)

WALKING TIME ALLOWANCE

3 hours

DISTANCE

9.0 km (5.6 miles)

TOTAL HEIGHT GAINED

90 m (295 ft)

HIGHEST POINT

Unnamed summit at MR 514655 — 85 m (280 ft)

digest/o/walk

PARKING

The ferry leaves from Cleggan (MR 602584) on the mainland. Park as close to the pier as possible and, when necessary, 'pay-to-park' on nearby private ground made available for that purpose by certain enterprising local people.

OVERVIEW/INTEREST

- The excursion starts and finishes with an enjoyable boat trip across the divide that separates Cleggan Bay and Bofin Harbour.
- Walk back in time to a place where visitors may sample life passing by at a more leisurely and agreeable pace.
- The walk explores the more rugged western aspects of delightful Inishbofin.
- Observe and explore a fascinating coastline that contains beaches, cliffs, sea arches and blowholes.
- Magnificent seascapes dotted with surrounding islands.

163

INISHBOFIN

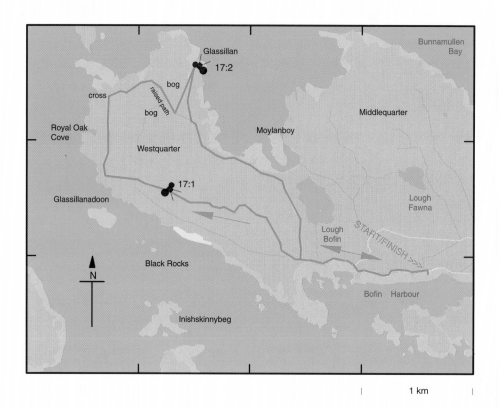

1 km

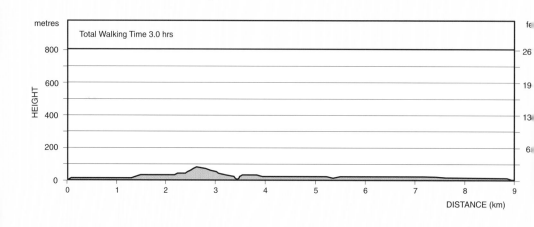

GRADIENTS

Following a walk along the shoreline, there is a gradual climb to the dominating summit located towards the westernmost point of the island. This involves gaining nearly 300 feet in height. Most of this is almost immediately surrendered and, thereafter, the rest of the route is fairly flat.

AMENITIES

There are hotels and refreshment facilities near to the disembarkation pier, dotted around Bofin Harbour.

MAPS, FOOTPATHS AND WAYSIGNS

OS DISCOVERY SERIES 1:50 000 — NUMBER 37 (MAYO AND GALWAY)

Much of the way is along either minor, surfaced roads or well-established, wide tracks. The highest ground traverses across open countryside where there are only intermittent, narrow paths, and part of the loop around the W and NW fringes of the island crosses rougher, boggier terrain where the route becomes rather obscure in a few places.

Signs, cairns and other markers are not plentiful, but with the coastline and sea in view for most of the way, route finding should not present any formidable difficulties.

GETTING STARTED

Abandon your vehicle at the small village of Cleggan on the mainland. Cleggan may be reached along any of several minor roads that lead westwards off the main N59 road that connects Clifden to the S with Letterfrack to the N. These approach roads pass through really lovely countryside and, if you have time, use them to make a circuit of the area, travelling down one on the way out and choosing an alternative one for your return journey.

Stepping off the boat on to dry land once more, make your way to the inland end of the substantial pier at Bofin Harbour, turn L and walk westwards, slightly uphill, along the minor road to pass Barrack Point, observed across the still waters of the sheltered bay.

ORGANISATION OF WALK AND ASSOCIATED EXCURSION

A day spent on Inishbofin will be constrained by the times of the ferry and alternative boat sailing schedules. When in the area, it will usually be possible to have breakfast at a normal hour and then to motor to Cleggan, without due haste, in order to catch one of the mid-morning sailings to the island. The return trip across the water may be delayed until the late afternoon, and this will allow ample time to complete the described walk and have some refreshments in unhurried comfort, before you reluctantly return to the pier to catch your boat back.

DESCRIPTION OF WALK

The first section of the walk leads you westwards along the attractive sound of Bofin Harbour, in whose protective embraces the main pier serving the island has been constructed. As you walk along, ahead on your L, a fascinating assortment of tiny islands and sea-stacks come into sight, and these together with the rocky headlands jutting out towards them combine to conjure up the most superb seascapes imaginable. Along here, the remaining structures of Cromwell's ruined fort also appear on the headland on the far side of the inlet, but as these may conjure up less savoury images, it is as well that you quickly press on past these remains. In front of you, attractive, rounded, green hills form the distant horizon towards which you are now heading.

⅄ 17:1 THE HIGH GROUND OF THE TWELVE PINS ON THE MAINLAND POSITIONED FROM THE HEIGHTS OF INISHBOFIN

Follow the narrow, winding road as it hugs the line of the seashore to pass by Emerald Cottage, near to which you must ignore a side turning off to the R. The continuation way then passes by a helicopter landing pad before reaching the attractively located Doonmore Hotel. Then walk past the next side turning leading off to the R and head uphill to walk past the last of the buildings in this vicinity, these an appealing assortment of old and new.

As further height is gained, Lough Bofin comes into view down on your R. (You will walk past this during your return.) Then fork R along a less well-used track, one which features a grassed-over, central reservation, still gaining incremental height. Along here you will obtain your first impressions of the rocky northern coastline of the island, and when you reach the next rise ahead, the full sweep of the sheltered bay flanked by the headland of Glassillan and the tiny island of Gubatarraghna makes an impressive appearance.

The way continues westwards, heading towards the higher ground ahead on your L. Keep faith with the track to where it terminates at a metal gate. Pass through this gateway and then climb the steeper, grassy slopes, still progressing W to reach the cairn positioned near the top of the hill. You will need to avoid some boggy patches on the way up. When you get to the cairn you will realise that this marks what is deemed a 'false top'! This is because from here you will now see a second cairn which positions the highest point of the hill, fortunately only slightly above your present elevation.

On reaching this second cairn you will have attained a height of about 85 m (280 ft), all of this under your own steam from sea level, and you will venture no higher than this during the remainder of the walk! In clear weather, the all-round panoramas from this hilly area, which is unnamed on the OS map, are simply fantastic. These take the form of the most perfect kaleidoscope of land and water, these ingredients skilfully shaken about to reveal in their midst the nearby island of Inishshark popping up above the waves to the W and the contrasting humped-back silhouette of holy Croagh Patrick mountain rising majestically in the distant NE, where it forms part of the mainland. In between these sightings, the high, rugged mountains of Co Mayo and Connemara, including the Mweelreas and The Twelve Pins, compete for your lingering attention.

Start your descent towards NW, heading towards the spur of ground that protrudes out to sea to form a rocky headland. Keep towards the crest of the broad, main ridge whilst walking down to pass by some tiny bog pools. Trim your line of descent to coincide with making use of the easier, grassy gullies to avoid unnecessarily tangling with any rocky outcrops and steeper sections. Finally, drop down a grassy channel on your L that will connect you with the paved cart track below.

Turn R along this easier and better defined way and follow it as it curves around to the R, passing by spectacular cliff faces visible over to your L. These form the rugged sides of an otherwise gentle, grassy headland. These arresting sights merit a closer inspection and a short detour to your L will enable you to do this. However, be extremely cautious when approaching the crumbling edges that line these steep fall-aways and do not venture too close to these, always keeping a tight grip of the wrists of any young children in your party!

Afterwards, return to the man-made track and bear L along it to then head NE, by-passing nasty-looking boglands below on your R. You will then pass by areas where turf cutting is still being performed by hand methods and you will need to skirt above these to the L, keeping to the better drained, grassy, higher ground and maintaining a northwards bearing. Cross over the slightly higher ground ahead to connect with a faint track and then head towards a prominent cross, mounted in a boulder. This is the vicinity of MR 507664 near the shoreline. When you get there, you will observe that this cross is made out of copper in an unusual, hollowed-out shape. The cross is a poignant memorial to a couple of

Americans from Kansas who over 20 years ago were trapped and drowned by the incoming tide whilst exploring the offshore rocks near here.

Just beyond the certain landmark of the cross, turn R from your direction of approach along a wide, stony track, now heading ENE quite close to the shore. The remnants of a sheep dip are then reached in an area of ground infested with rabbit burrows. From here, keep to the surfaced track as it leads you SE. This is along a raised way that threads through treacherous, oozy bog on either side, which definitely needs to be avoided! When you eventually reach firmer ground ahead, turn off your secure track to the L to cross rocky ground in order to view the spectacular sea arch and blowhole configuration (described as Subterranean Passage on the OS map) ahead. Scramble down over the jumble of rocks but exercise care doing so, especially when these rocks are wet and slippery.

Afterwards, make your way back to the track, passing by a marker cairn constructed of turf *en route* there. From here, a faintly defined path leads initially S heading towards the secure ground of the raised, stony way that you departed from earlier. Turn L along this track, changing your direction of travel to SE to then pass between enclosing walling that funnels you past an isolated sheep farm. From here, just continue along the walled way.

The return route then passes above a stony beach, after which you pass through a metal gate that you are requested to shut after use. The way then winds back towards denser habitation in the shape of a line of cottages positioned just above the seashore. The route then turns inland to pass along the western side of Lough Bofin, which you looked down on earlier in the day. Turn L at the end of the track and retrace your outward steps back towards the harbour. If you have sufficient time you may decide to allow the ambience and refreshments served at the Doonmore Hotel to delay your arrival there!

SUITABILITY OF WALK AND ASSOCIATED PLACES OF INTEREST FOR FAMILIES

The suitability of this walk is very much dependent upon the weather. When conditions are fine, most older children will enjoy the full way described, even though this involves some climbing and the crossing of patches of rougher, boggy ground. Those of you with smaller children have two choices. One is to venture up towards the higher ground near the start of the walk described, in order to observe the fine views from here given favourable weather, before retracing your steps back towards the harbour. The alternative is to explore the last part of the described route, by walking towards or even reaching the spectacular sea arch and blowholes, before once again retreating the way you came.

⋀ **17:2** GUIDE CHRISTOPHER STACEY ADDING SIZE DIMENSION TO A SEA CAVE ON THE NORTH-WEST COAST OF INISHBOFIN

PLACES OF INTEREST

INISHBOFIN

This irregular-shaped island, some $5\frac{1}{2}$ km ($3\frac{1}{2}$ miles) long, E to W, by some $3\frac{1}{2}$ km ($2\frac{1}{4}$ miles) wide at its broadest point, lies about 8 km (5 miles) along a ferry crossing from the tiny coastal village of Cleggan on the mainland. A boat trip to the island followed by stretching your legs across its attractive, undulating hillsides makes a splendid day out given fine weather, and this could well seduce you into making a longer visit to the island on some future occasion. The local people you come into contact with will make you feel very welcome and you will soon become immersed in the quaint charm and leisurely pace of life that are such endearing features of the place. There are sheltered beaches, spectacular cliffs and modestly sized green hills to explore, and time spent there will almost certainly pass by all too quickly for most day-trippers. Just to fill in any odd moments, other possibilities include observing seals, watching whales, visiting archaeological sites dating back to the Iron Age, discovering rare flora and fauna, and identifying the island's extensive bird life.

For sailings and departure times of the ferry and boat services from Cleggan to Inishbofin, contact:

Paddy O'Halloran (Skipper)
The Mailboat
Dun Aengus
Tel: 095 45806
(Tickets available at Spar Foodstore,
Cleggan, Connemara, Co Galway
Tel: 095 44750)

Kings of Cleggan
Connemara
Co Galway
Tel: 095 44642
Fax: 095 44327

169

KYLEMORE ABBEY

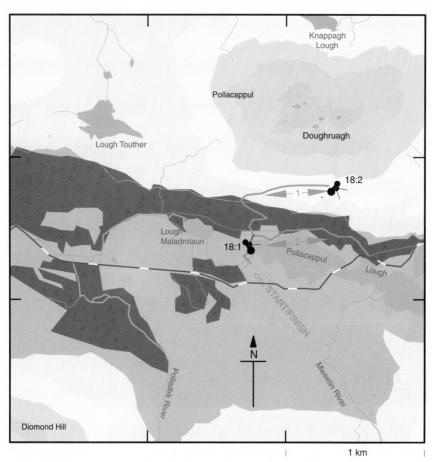

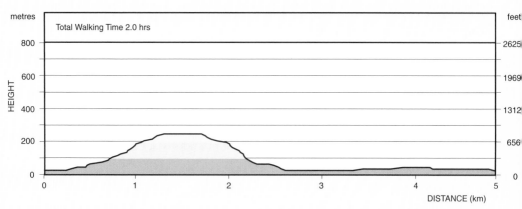

KYLEMORE ABBEY

fact*f*ile

START/FINISH
Kylemore Abbey car park — MR 747583

GRADING
Easy/straightforward (colour-coded BLUE)

WALKING TIME ALLOWANCE
2 hours

DISTANCE
5.0 km (3.1 miles)

TOTAL HEIGHT GAINED
240 m (785 ft)

HIGHEST POINT
Statue positioned on slopes of Doughruagh — 250 m (820 ft)

digest *o*f walk

PARKING
Large and well-organised parking facilities catering for large inflow of visitors to Kylemore Abbey.

OVERVIEW/INTEREST

- Visit to and exploration of a major tourist attraction.
- Magnificent, rugged setting amongst lakes and mountains galore.
- Combination of two walks, an energetic climb to a lofty statue and a leisurely stroll by the side of a picturesque lake.
- Abbey, visitor centre, video studio, statue, mausoleum and church all compete for your attention.
- Superb views across Kylemore Lough towards the Maumturk Mountains and in the other direction down along a delightfully wooded valley towards the coast.

The climb up to the statue is steep along a rough path that zigzags up the rugged mountainside. By complete contrast, the walk by the side of sheltered Pollacappul Lough is virtually on the flat.

Toilets, excellent refreshment facilities, a well-stocked gift shop and an audiovisual centre are located at the abbey.

OS DISCOVERY SERIES 1:50 000 — NUMBER 37 (MAYO AND GALWAY)

The steep climb up to the statue is along a rough path surfaced with stones. There are some wet areas along here due to the fact that several small watercourses cross your way up. By contrast, the walk down to the E gate to visit the church and other sites is along a wide, well-maintained way.

There are plenty of directional signs within the grounds of the abbey.

Kylemore Abbey is situated at the western end of Kylemore Lough, just off the main N59 road that connects Westport to the NE with Clifden to the SW.

From the extensive parking area, cross over the river by the bridge and make your way to the visitor centre, following the helpful directional signs.

ORGANISATION OF WALK AND ASSOCIATED EXCURSION

Allow at least half a day to complete the two short walks suggested, to have a good look around Kylemore Abbey with its many visitor attractions, to see the interesting video presentation and to allow time for some delicious refreshments to be consumed there without undue haste.

DESCRIPTION OF WALK

Having paid your entry fee, walk towards the abbey, but before you reach these imposing buildings, branch L to then walk uphill along the internal road, signed 'International Girls School — School Entrance Only'. (Do not be put off by the second part of this sign, as you are not going there, that is unless you just happen to be one of the pupils!) When you reach the top of the entrance drive, bear L up the steps following the way signed 'Path to Statue'. Shortly after this, another more sombre sign is reached that reads 'Visitors use this path at their own risk'. Please heed this sensible warning, tread with care and look after any children that are with you.

Then fork immediately L to mount more steps that lead you steeply up through pervading rhododendron shrubbery. A rough, stony path winds further up the mountainside from the top of the steps, passing through enclosing woodlands and under the branches of more rhododendron bushes. Distant visibility is non-existent as you pass through this dense tangle of foliage. However, this will allow you to concentrate on avoiding a number of tiny watercourses that trickle across your way, these gurgling merrily as they flow down the steep hillsides up which your way is snaking.

Just keep progressing upwards along the obvious path, choosing a rate of climb that suits you best. Higher up, as the trees fan out, there are tantalising glimpses through gaps in the foliage of the northernmost aspects of The Twelve Pins, and the distinctive, pointed shapes of Diomond Hill (or Bengooria) and Benbaun may be identified to SW and SE respectively. Further up, be careful to avoid a stub turning on your R by keeping to the main track that then bends sharply in that direction.

Further up still, and quite suddenly (given clear weather), the most magnificent panoramic views open up on your R. These are down across the abbey and its lakes towards the grandeur of the mighty, pointed peaks of The Twelve Pins. These pearly-grey, quartzite mountains rise steeply to the SSE on the far side of the intervening, glaciated valley. Take particular care of any young children that are with you along this stretch due to the steep fall-away quite close to your and, more pertinently, their feet!

Then you are there, standing close to the statue which is set on an elevated plinth. The white edifice is about 12 ft high and is named 'Sacred Heart'. It was placed there on the instigation of the nuns of the abbey in 1932 and is said to have been carried up the steep mountainside in one piece by 16 local men; obviously these stalwarts were of the superman variety! Quite apart from the interest of the statue, the views from this position, given favourable weather, are superb. To the E beyond the sheltered waters of Kylemore Lough the profile of the rugged Maumturk Mountains forms a riveting skyline, whilst in the opposite direction the vistas are along a delightful, deciduously wooded valley that trains the eyes towards the distant coastline. In between these features, the craggy, northern slopes of The Twelve Pins rise majestically to the S, completing a semi-circle of the most wonderful mountainous scenery imaginable.

Return the way you came, now walking steeply downhill towards the considerable amenities of the abbey waiting for you below.

The second part of the walk is along the way that leads to the E gate of the estate, passing by the wooded shores of lovely Pollacappul Lough. Along here a fine Gothic church may be visited.

To start this section of the ramble, select the way signed 'Lake Walk to Gothic Church' to pass between the abbey and the northern shores of Pollacappul Lough. Bear R ahead to hug the attractively wooded shoreline of the lake where a number of named, specimen trees have been planted.

The fine Gothic church is soon reached and you can either stop to have a look inside now or delay this pleasure until your return. Continue on along the way now signed 'Mausoleum' to penetrate more natural woodlands which contain a mixture of mature beech, chestnut, oak and sycamore trees. Then cross over a stream by means of a bridge to reach the mausoleum, this partly hidden away amongst the foliage on your L. Again you have a choice of when to inspect this more closely.

Continue as far as the E gate in order to observe the splendid views across Kylemore Lough towards the distant Maumturks. Beech trees shade the delightful shores of the lough in this vicinity. When you have seen enough, return the way you came back to the visitor centre and other amenities, visiting the mausoleum, church and abbey *en route* if you have not already done so, once more savouring the tranquillity of the delightful woodland scenery as you make your way back. You will find the interior of the Gothic church stunningly simple, with the roof supported by beautiful lierne vaulting and a fine, stained-glass window decorating the south transept. Also during your return make sure you see the nuns' enclosure and shrine; this is off to the R near the abbey.

SUITABILITY OF WALK AND ASSOCIATED PLACES OF INTEREST FOR FAMILIES

A prolonged visit to Kylemore Abbey will be irresistible for most families when either staying in the area or just passing by the gates. There is much to interest everybody here, and I am confident all will thoroughly enjoy both their exploration of the man-made constructions located here — both old and new — and also relaxing amongst the magnificent natural scenery of the extensive, wooded estate.

The climb up to the statue is not suitable for very young children due to both its difficulty and the several steep, potentially dangerous fall-aways that line this route higher up. Everyone, even those being pushed along, should enjoy the short meander through the woodlands in close proximity to the gently lapping waters of the lough.

PLACES OF INTEREST

KYLEMORE ABBEY
Kylemore Abbey has been tastefully developed into a major tourist attraction, skilfully blending its interesting heritage and magnificent location with the modern amenities that discerning visitors nowadays demand.

The abbey is situated within the heart of the majestic Connemara mountains, along a lovely wooded valley just over a kilometre to the W of Kylemore Lough. It has been the home of the enterprising Irish Benedictine nuns since 1920, but it was originally built as a castle by Mitchell Henry, a textile industrialist born in Manchester, England, as a gift for his wife Margaret, to whom he was devoted. Trees and the abbey are synonymous, for the correct Irish spelling of Kylemore is Coill Mór, which translated is 'Big Wood'.

An international girls' boarding school is located at the abbey and an exhibition of the colourful history of the estate is on view in some of the restored reception rooms of the abbey which have been opened to the public. One of the main attractions is the restored Gothic church, a building of international

△ **18:2** THE VIEW FROM THE HIGH POINT OF THE WALK TOWARDS KYLEMORE LOUGH AND BENBAUN

significance that is famed as a miniature cathedral, this complete with stained-glass windows, marble columns and intricate stone carvings.

The Victorian garden, located a mile or so to the W of the abbey, is currently being restored to its former glory. The intention is that paths will be opened up through the intervening deciduous woodlands to enable visitors to walk at leisure from the formal part of the estate to this protected, walled sanctuary which will eventually comprise geometric flower beds, a kitchen garden and a glasshouse complex, these covering in all some six acres.

The visitor amenities include a restaurant where delicious home cooking may be sampled; a craft shop owned and managed by the nuns where quality goods (knitwear, pottery, crystal, jewellery etc.), some exclusively designed for the abbey, may be purchased; a pottery studio where craftspeople at work may be observed; and a theatre where an interesting video of the history of the estate may be viewed in comfort. Information leaflets on all aspects of the abbey and the estate are available from the information desks.

For further details contact:

Kylemore Abbey
Connemara
Co Galway
Tel: 095 41146
Fax: 095 41123

ERRISBEG (AND ROUNDSTONE)

fact file

START/FINISH
Parking lay-by near centre of village — MR 724402

GRADING
Moderate/challenging (colour-coded RED)

WALKING TIME ALLOWANCE
3.5 hours

DISTANCE
7.6 km (4.7 miles)

TOTAL HEIGHT GAINED
310 m (1015 ft)

HIGHEST POINT
Errisbeg — 300 m (985 ft)

digest of walk

PARKING
Ample parking in the centre of Roundstone, near to the post office.

OVERVIEW/INTEREST
- Walk commences from the attractive coastal village of Roundstone with its picturesque harbour.
- Fantastic panoramas for most of the way, both of surrounding seascapes and towards the distant Twelve Pins.
- Isolated mountain provides a bird's-eye view of the extensive, low-lying boglands to the NW.
- Interesting rock formations and several separate mini-peaks to scale.
- Chance of a swim or paddle on the nearby sandy beaches of Dogs Bay and Gorteen Bay.

Errisbeg (and Roundstone)

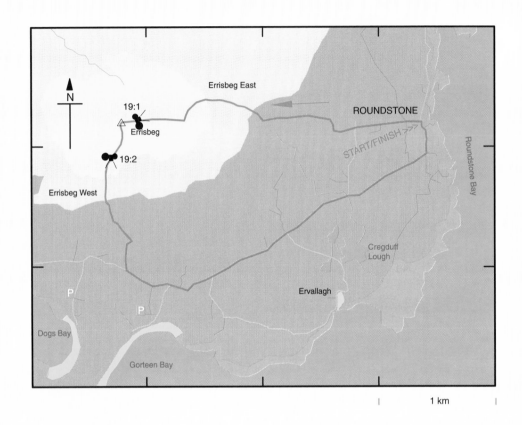

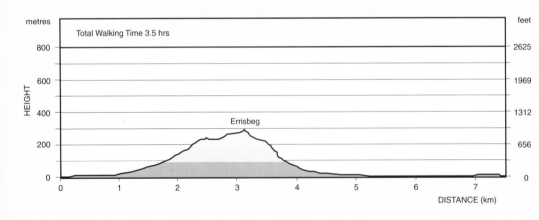

GRADIENTS

From just above sea level, the way is continuously uphill for the best part of a thousand feet. The initial approach is gentle but the slopes steepen significantly and become more rugged towards the extensive summit area of the mountain. This process is reversed on the way down, with steeper, craggy ground near the top giving way to less formidable, grassy slopes lower down.

AMENITIES

Plenty of hotels, guest houses, bars and restaurants to suit all tastes in Roundstone.

MAPS, FOOTPATHS AND WAYSIGNS

OS DISCOVERY SERIES 1:50 000 — NUMBER 44 (GALWAY)

The start and finish of the route are along minor roads and well-defined tracks. Once on open ground on the slopes of the mountain, paths become rather scarce and much of the way is across and up and down uncharted, rough terrain with only a few sheep tracks and the occasional stretch of narrow path to guide you. There are some boggy areas, especially so on the way up and towards the end of the descent, but these may quite easily be avoided with some careful forward planning of where you go next.

Signs, apart from along the roads, are non-existent! However, a series of cairns marks most of the high spots in the extensive, undulating summit area of Errisbeg.

GETTING STARTED

The village of Roundstone is located on the R341 road that loops through it. The village may be approached along this road either from Clifden to the NW or from the NE by turning off the main N59 road at Canal Bridge (MR 803474).

On foot, leave the village along the side road that leads upwards to the W, commencing along the side of O'Dowd's Restaurant and Seafood Bar opposite the harbour.

ORGANISATION OF WALK AND ASSOCIATED EXCURSION

You really would need to allow a full day to drive along the scenic, indented coastline to reach Roundstone, to complete the walk in comfort, possibly to spend some time on the beach and perhaps even to finish the trip off in style by having a meal in one of the renowned restaurants in the village that specialise in serving delicious dishes of freshly caught fish.

Try to choose a day when visibility is good, because the extensive summit area of Errisbeg can be very confusing in misty conditions and, in any case, fine weather is needed to observe the extensive views at their best.

DESCRIPTION OF WALK

Walk straight past the first turning on your R and then also ignore the road leading off on the L that serves the bungalows located there. Instead, keep heading W along the narrow lane making directly towards the craggy slopes rising ahead. This higher ground leads to the vast summit area of Errisbeg, your principal objective for the walk. Do not deviate from this approach when you reach a crossroads ahead; just keep straight on along a rougher continuation track, still proceeding W and gaining height at a modest rate.

⋏ **19:1** The rough ground connecting the several craggy summits of Errisbeg

The lane terminates at a superbly located cottage that has been tastefully renovated and is now available for holiday rental. Local farmer Tom O'Dowell, or his representative, is the person you need to see about this. Go through the wooden gate just above the cottage to enter open countryside and then contour up the rough, stony path, walking by the side of a hedge on your L.

Further up, veer away from the hedge, keeping to the R of a tiny stream and following the course of a narrow path that leads uphill beside the trickling water. Maintain your established westwards bearing, keeping to a less obviously defined way that crosses a number of wet and boggy areas. Fortunately, a clearer path intermittently surfaced with rocks and grass soon becomes re-established and this will lead you across another stream. Turn around along here to marvel at the magnificent seascapes that are now visible, given clear weather. The village of Roundstone is spread-eagled below you to the E, with the irregular shape of Bertraghboy Bay revealing its considerable secrets way beyond, whilst the high peaks of The Twelve Pins may be identified, miles away to the NE.

The path continues to rise, passing by clumps of gorse, which are seen at their colourful best when in full bloom in late April and May. Then further up still, be careful to aim for the L side of a wide, shallow hause that looms up ahead to the NW. Your approach to this passes over a number of tiny watercourses. Select a diagonal track that hugs the higher ground and, bearing slightly to the L, thread a route of your own choice up the steeper, rockier slopes that rise to the L. You should then connect with a faint path-cum-watercourse that you may conveniently tread along to maintain your established diagonal, bearing further L again higher up.

There are now, given favourable weather, excellent views to your R rear, and these progressively reveal the fuller topography of The Twelve Pins and the more immediate surrounding seascapes as you gain further, incremental height. Keep your heading between NW and WNW for the time being, still climbing and taking care to thread the easiest passage through the heathers and around the rocky crags and circumventing the worst of all wet and boggy patches.

Continue to seek out the higher ground, now bearing further to the L to assume a more westwards direction of progress and to pass through a somewhat confusing area of small hillocks that protrude from the main slopes of the rugged mountainside. A small pool should then be passed, but do not become unduly concerned if the precise route you have selected does not bring this into view! Then, with perhaps some relief, over an outcrop of rock ahead, the craggy profile of the E summit ridge of Errisbeg will be revealed. Drop down to cross the intervening grassy gully to get there, treading around some boggy ground on the way.

The final section of your approach to the E summit area, across easier ground and up more gently rising slopes, is less demanding. Ahead of you now are a number of rocky hillocks, each one marked by a tiny cairn — visit them all provided the weather is kind and you have sufficient time, for the different perspectives from each of these is well worth the small, extra effort in getting there. In particular, the new vistas of the extensive, low-lying, boggy wastelands stretching away for miles to the NW are just fantastic. A few words of warning: in misty weather be careful to steer well clear of a deep cleft at the bottom of a slab of rock on the L, easterly pinnacle. This hazard is usually filled with water and is definitely a place where not to place either of your feet!

To continue, thread your way with care down the rocky slope to then bisect the shallow hause separating you from the main summit area of Errisbeg. This rises a short distance further WSW. When climbing again, track around to the L in order to avoid steep cliff faces and huge boulders to the R! A more substantial cairn is then reached, and from here, providing you are not enveloped in mist, the main summit trigonometrical point may be observed rising across rough, rocky terrain a short distance further W. Walk there, crossing another intervening craggy hause in the process.

The main summit of Errisbeg commands a height of 300 m (985 ft) and, given fine weather, the all-round panoramas from this modest but isolated summit are breathtaking. Most of the highlights in these extensive vistas have already been positioned but there are now extensive new views S towards the coast. Here, the fascinating promontory of low-lying, green land that separates the two attractive sweeps of sand lining Dogs Bay and Gorteen Bay may be observed. It is towards this landmark to the SSW that you will be aiming during your subsequent descent.

Start going down heading towards these sandy beaches and searching out all easier ground that leads SSW. You will come to some steep, awkward sections, but spot these before you get there and just plan a way down that avoids them, always maintaining a southward bearing. Good use may be made of a series of easier, grassy clefts and channels that twist between the more formidable large boulders and rock benches. A certain amount of weaving about will be necessary, but just take your time, constantly looking ahead to select beforehand the easiest passage down through each discrete section of the way.

Much lower down, trim your descent to reach the stone walling below at a point where there is a junction with another wall leading off at right angles. Cross the walling with care at this low point and then continue your descent beside the walling on your L. You now have to cross some exacting boggy ground as you thread your way gingerly through clumps of prickly gorse. Then pass through a convenient gap in the walling directly ahead of you to continue downhill across more boggy ground before crossing the next walling at another low point.

Turn R when you reach the boundary walling of a house below and proceed through the gap in the next wall. Then follow the boundary walling further down, keeping this on your L. This will lead you directly to a metal gate that provides access to a wide track below. Turn R to continue heading down the final gentle slope as the way leads through more metal gates to reach the road below. (Note: When last visited, the final descent area was being developed with more properties and it may be that when this is completed the way through this section may be slightly changed; if in doubt as to the correct way, please seek advice from the helpful residents. I did just this to confirm that part of the route described here!)

Turn L along the R341 road and head back towards Roundstone, some 3 km (nearly 2 miles) away to the NE, virtually on the flat all the way! If you wish to return direct, ignore all side roads as you walk along, including one signed to 'Gurteen Bay Caravan and Camping Park'. Otherwise, you may visit the nearby, fine beaches and an out-of-town Information Point *en route*.

⋏ **19:2** PAUSE ON THE WAY DOWN FROM THE SUMMIT OF ERRISBEG TO TAKE IN THE VIEW TOWARDS DOGS BAY AND GORTEEN BAY BELOW

SUITABILITY OF WALK AND ASSOCIATED PLACES OF INTEREST FOR FAMILIES

Families with older children, including sturdy teenagers who are experienced walkers, should enjoy this challenging short walk when the weather is clear and fine. Those with younger children are advised to stick to the lower ground and spend their time in and about Roundstone, where they can enjoy themselves and relax on the nearby, sheltered, sandy beaches.

PLACES OF INTEREST

ROUNDSTONE

The small seaside village of Roundstone is a popular holiday resort during the summer months when it is all hustle and bustle along its narrow, main street. It is not hard to comprehend why this is so. The town is splendidly located on the sheltered, western shores of picturesque Bertraghboy Bay. From here there are the most superb views north-eastwards towards the high mountains of Connemara. The tiny harbour has been described as one of the prettiest along the western seaboard, and nearby there are vast sweeps of uncrowded, clean, golden sand. These tiny granules are a children's paradise.

Visitors are well catered for, with a variety of hotels, guest houses, rented accommodation and caravan sites, and the town boasts a wide range of pubs and restaurants to suit all tastes, particularly those of fish gourmets. An Arts Week is held in early July where new paintings and sculptures, some by local artists, are exhibited. These viewings are buttressed with traditional music, plays, slide shows, book launches (now there's a thought!), fashion shows, walks, field trips, concerts and workshops. Then on the second day . . .

Just for the record, the name Roundstone is an English corruption of Cloch na Rón, which means 'The Stone of the Seal', and the village and harbour were built in the early nineteenth century by Alexander Nimmo, a Scottish engineer, appropriately enough for Scottish fishermen.

For further information contact:

Roundstone Information Centre
Errisbeg House
Roundstone
Connemara
Co Galway
Tel: 095 35834
Mobile phone: 086 8215153
Fax: 095 35715
Email: marquis@connemara.net

CROAGH PATRICK (AND WESTPORT HOUSE)

fact/ile

START/FINISH
Murrisk — MR 919823

GRADING
Moderate/challenging (colour-coded RED)

WALKING TIME ALLOWANCE
4 hours

DISTANCE
6.8 km (4.2 miles)

TOTAL HEIGHT GAINED
770 m (2525 ft)

HIGHEST POINT
Croagh Patrick — 764 m (2505 ft)

digest/o walk

PARKING
Extensive car-parking facilities, adjacent to R335 road.

OVERVIEW/INTEREST
- Follow the Pilgrim's Path to the top of holy Croagh Patrick.
- Stand on top of the most climbed mountain in the whole of Ireland.
- Opportunity to reflect, pray, give thanks and discharge penances.
- Magnificent coastal scenery in which the views across Clew Bay reign supreme.
- Opportunity to count up to 365 separate islands below you!

CROAGH PATRICK
(AND WESTPORT HOUSE)

 20:1

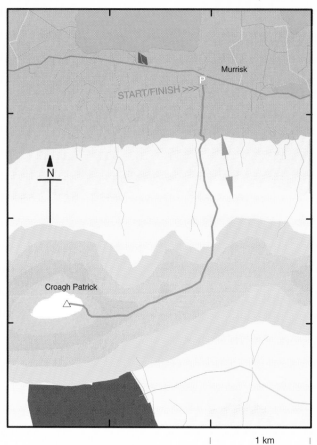

Murrisk

START/FINISH >>>

P

N

Croagh Patrick

1 km

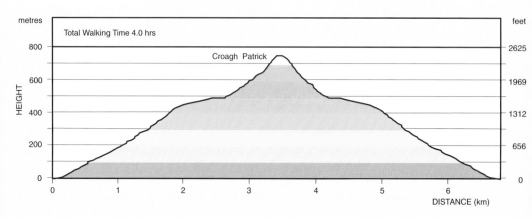

GRADIENTS

The route is one prolonged up and down. The slopes of Croagh Patrick are moderate to steep, and towards the summit there are places where the severity of the gradient and the rough, unstable scree render the route a challenging experience.

AMENITIES

Toilet facilities are located at the parking area and also in two places on the mountain.

MAPS, FOOTPATHS AND WAYSIGNS

OS DISCOVERY SERIES 1:50 000 — NUMBERS 30, 31, 37 AND 38 (MAYO AND GALWAY)

A wide, eroded path snakes all the way to the top of the mountain and anybody who gets lost when following this should seriously consider giving up hillwalking! The going underfoot is invariably rough and in a few places extreme when climbing steep scree slopes that demand sensible footwear.

Most of the signs are religious ones but no waymarkers should be needed to get safely to the top and back.

GETTING STARTED

Murrisk lies on the R335 coastal road that links Westport with Louisburgh. The car park for the walk is located about 8 km (5 miles) W of Westport.

Make your way across to the toilet block and from here follow the obvious, walled path to the R that leads gently up the slope towards SSW. At the far end, turn R up the surfaced road and you are pointing and walking towards the lower slopes of Croagh Patrick, straight ahead of you. Fuchsia bushes abound along this quiet, pleasant, initial approach.

ORGANISATION OF WALK AND ASSOCIATED EXCURSION

The climb up and down should not take more than about half a day and so during the longest days of summer you can combine this with doing other things whilst in the area. Early morning and mid to late afternoon are good times to set out during this period in order to observe the sunrise or sunset respectively. Other things to do could include a visit to nearby Westport House.

Description of Walk

In clear weather you can see much of Croagh Patrick from the vicinity of the parking area, its huge bulk rising to the SW. In these conditions, part of the route snaking up there may also be identified and so right from the start you are able to assess what lies above you! In the opposite direction is Clew Bay, but for the time being most of this is obscured from view.

Bear R at the top of the lane to access the start of the rough, eroded path that bears the scars of the 'multitudes on the mount' before you! A statue of St Patrick straddles the path a short distance ahead and this provides details for those making a pilgrimage out of the walk. Continue climbing along the obvious, wide path heading southwards up the mountain.

As you gain height, fantastic views begin to appear behind you of Clew Bay and of the mountains beyond to the NW. These heights almost automatically direct your gaze westwards out to sea towards Achill Island. Tiny islands also litter the bay and it is contended that at low tide there is one of these for each day of the year. (The author has never counted anywhere near this prodigious number, but then he does not normally carry a chart of the tides!)

The route you are using is named 'The Pilgrim's Path' for obvious reasons and you are asked to respect the sacredness of this holy place. This path is over stones, rocks and boulders, parts of which, after heavy rains, have to be shared with running water! Beyond a ramshackle, wooden gate, a steeper gradient stretches ahead as the way snakes further uphill keeping company with the course of a tumbling stream to your R. The path will then bring you to a wide hause that is located along the main E to W axis of the mountain. On the final part of the climb to the hause the attractive, white-painted buildings and outlying farms of Westport come into view to the E, whilst in the opposite direction, beyond the shoulder of the mountain, part of Clare Island may be observed.

You can allow yourself a short respite after having accomplished the connection with the main spur, for the next section of the way is fairly level as you swing around to the R to then continue by heading westwards. When walking across this easier ground you will pass by a small shelter. As you complete this stretch whilst getting your breath back, wild and wonderful landscapes filled with forests, lakes and rivers open up far below you on your L towards the S, that is assuming good visibility. Beyond this absorbing wilderness, the ground rises again to form the Sheeffry Hills and the Mweelrea Mountains.

Slight undulations are taken in your stride as another shelter and then a toilet block come and go. A third shelter is passed, and after this the first pilgrimage station of 'Leacht Benain' is reached; devout walkers get a chance to become dizzy here, circling around the large cairn of stones while voicing their prayers.

The continued ascent then reaches steeper ground where more difficult, loose scree slopes have to be conquered. About 400 paces (some 300 m) further on, be vigilant to locate and turn off up a narrower side path to the R. This deviation from the main track avoids the worst of some exacting, steep terrain ahead which is covered with awkwardly sized, loose scree. It will also disassociate you, for some distance, from most other people on the mountainside and more importantly from those above you who might dislodge stones and rocks that could then roll down and strike you! This temporarily changes your direction of ascent to NW as you climb higher across unstable slopes but along a narrow, clearly defined path that hugs a relatively secure ledge. When you reach a junction ahead, turn L to continue further uphill. Your diversion then reconnects with the much busier, main way up a short distance further on. Turn R here into the denser traffic stream of human endeavour. A pointed stone marks this important junction, and this place should be committed to memory for instant recall on the way down.

Be extra careful from here on as you climb up the more eroded, steeper, slippery slopes and do watch out for the mistakes of others, particularly those made by people above you, some of whom, clad in totally unsuitable footwear such as pumps and sandals, are apt to slither about out of control all over the place, dislodging stones and fragments of rock as they involuntarily do so.

The sighting of buildings ahead signals that you have almost made it to the top, so you can prepare to relax your vigilance. Almost immediately after this you will reach the second pilgrimage station, appropriately enough named 'The Summit', where you may again witness walkers going around in circles. The trigonometrical point lies just a few feet beyond this. Then a surprisingly large, white-painted church is reached a short distance further W. I have never found it open yet on several visits up there, but it does make an exceedingly efficient wind-block and I put it to good use for this purpose on more than one occasion! Toilets are also located on the top and these are usually available for instant use.

The large and interesting summit area of Croagh Patrick commands a height of 764 m (2505 ft) and, because the mountain stands alone, this elevated viewing position commands unrestricted views of the countryside all around when the weather is fine. Most of the highlights in these have previously been positioned and you are left here to observe and recapitulate these at your leisure.

When you have feasted enough on these panoramic views, start your descent the way you came, but this time heading ESE. From here, simply retrace your outward steps all the way back to the car park, when necessary being mindful of those below you by taking care not to dislodge any stones. On the way down be careful to locate and use again the side loop, now on your L, to avoid a particularly difficult section of descent. (Look out for that pointed marker stone that marks the spot where you need to turn off the main path.) Once on this lesser used way, be careful to turn R part way down before the way straight ahead simply peters out on the rough, inhospitable hillside.

When you reach the broad hause below, just past the first pilgrimage station, turn L down the eroded way and follow the wide track back past the large statue of St Patrick to the parking area below.

Suitability of Walk and Associated Places of Interest for Families

This fairly challenging climb is unsuitable for most younger children, although many of these do reach the top in fairly good heart! My advice is leave this walk until they are older; but, if you find the temptation of attempting to climb this holy mountain with young children too difficult to resist, start out properly clad, that is wearing boots and with sensible protective clothing with you, and see how far you get, always being prepared to turn back before the children complain that they have had enough!

PLACES OF INTEREST

CROAGH PATRICK

In A.D. 441, St Patrick is purported to have spent 40 days and nights praying, meditating and fasting on the top of this exposed mountain. However, at most times of the year, if you manage more than 40 seconds up there you will have done really well! The objective of the dedicated saint's sacrifice was to convert Ireland to Christianity. The mountain is the most climbed one in Ireland and possibly also in the entire universe! There is an annual pilgrimage up the mountain, which is held on the last Sunday in July and called Reek Sunday. Then, many thousands climb to the top, some all the way there in their bare feet! Obviously, depending upon how you feel about it, this is a date either to be there or to avoid at all costs! The place of devotion on the summit of Croagh Patrick was built in 1905, with materials for its construction being transported up there on the backs of donkeys. The church took a year to complete at a cost of £100, and the craftsmen and apprentices who built it endured long spells on the windswept summit with only a tent for protection!

WESTPORT HOUSE

Westport House Country Estate has been developed into a major tourist attraction, with the house, a splendid building located in a magnificent setting, protecting contents that have a strong west of Ireland association. Here there are fine ceilings by Richard Cassels and the dining-room designed by James Wyatt is considered to be amongst the finest in Ireland. Hand-painted Chinese wallpaper and Waterford Glass chandeliers feature prominently amongst the other prized exhibits.

The extensive gardens contain a children's zoo and one of the fun attractions located there is an express train, whilst sports facilities include a pitch and putt golf course, tennis and boating. A leisurely visit to this historic house will make a splendid day out for people of all ages.

For further information contact:

Westport House Country Estate
Westport
Co Mayo
Tel: 098 27766

SUMMARY OF WALKING ROUTES

This table provides a concise statistical summary of the 20 walking routes included in this book listed in numerical sequence.

Walk No	Name of Walk	Grading		Walking Time	Walking Distance		Total Height Gained		Highest Point	
		Easy/straight-forward	Moderate/challenging	hours	km	miles	metres	feet	metres	feet
1	Black Hill (and Pollaphuca Reservoir)		*	3.5	7.7	4.8	330	1085	602	1975
2	Great Sugar Loaf (and Powerscourt House etc.)	*	*	1.5	2.7	1.7	210	690	501	1645
3	Glendalough, Pollanass Waterfall and The Spink		*	3.5	8.3	5.2	360	1180	420	1380
4	Trooperstown Hill (and Avondale and Mount Usher)		*	4.0	9.7	6.0	400	1310	430	1410
5	Sugarloaf Hill and Bay Lough (and Mount Melleray)		*	3.0	6.1	3.8	420	1380	663	2175
6	Upper Nire Valley (and Tooreen Archaeological Site)	*		4.0	11.1	6.9	260	855	300	985
7	Coumshingaun Lough	*	*	2.5	4.1	2.5	290	950	400	1310
8	Pulleen Loop near Ardgroom (and Healy Pass)	*		2.0	5.1	3.2	140	460	65	215
9	Comnagapple Glen Circuit (and Bear Island)	*		3.0	7.2	4.5	230	755	240	785
10	Garinish Strand and Ballaghboy (and Dursey/Allihies)	*	*	2.5	5.7	3.5	210	690	151	495
11	Ross Island and Castle (and Killarney)	*		2.5	6.5	4.0	50	165	20	65
12	Seefin (and Kerry Bog Village Museum)		*	6.0	13.5	8.4	590	1935	493	1615
13	Skellig Rocks (and Skellig Heritage Centre)	*		—	1.2	0.7	170	560	170	560
14	Lough Anscaul and the Glennahoo Valley (and beach)		*	3.5	8.5	5.3	290	950	370	1215
15	Ballydavid Head (and the Blasket Islands)	*		2.5	6.0	3.7	240	785	247	810
16	Mount Eagle (and Oceanworld Aquarium)		*	3.5	7.6	4.7	510	1675	516	1695
17	Inishbofin	*		3.0	9.0	5.6	90	295	85	280
18	Kylemore Abbey	*		2.0	5.0	3.1	240	785	250	820
19	Errisbeg (and Roundstone)		*	3.5	7.6	4.7	310	1015	300	985
20	Croagh Patrick (and Westport House)		*	4.0	6.8	4.2	770	2525	764	2505
	Total				139.4	86.5	6110	20045		

USEFUL ADDRESSES

Contact information for selected walking guides, accommodation and places of interest is provided in the appropriate sections of the book. Listed here is additional, more general, contact information that may prove useful to walkers and visitors either before they go to Ireland or whilst there.

Automobile Association
23 Rock Hill
Blackrock
Co Dublin
Tel: 01 283 3555
Fax: 01 283 3660

Bus Éireann (Irish Bus)
Broadstone
Dublin 7
Tel: 01 830 2222
Fax: 01 830 9377
Email: info@buseireann.ie
Web site: www.buseireann.ie

Iarnród Éireann (Irish Rail)
Connolly Station
Dublin 1
Tel: 01 836 3333
Fax: 01 836 4760
Web site: www.irishrail.ie

Independent Holiday Hostels
57 Lower Gardiner Street
Dublin 1
Tel: 01 836 4700
Fax: 01 836 4710

Irish Country Holidays
5 Lord Edward Court
Bride Street
Dublin 8
Tel: 01 475 1257
Fax: 01 475 1258
Email: info@country-holidays.ie

Irish Farm Holidays
2 Michael Street
Limerick
Tel: 061 400700
Fax: 061 400771
Email: farmhols@iol.ie

Irish Hotels Federation
13 Northbrook Road
Dublin 6
Tel: 01 497 6459
Fax: 01 497 4613
Email: info@ihf.ie

Mountaineering Council of Ireland
c/o Association for Adventure Sports
House of Sport
Long Mile Road
Dublin 12
Tel: 01 450 9845
Fax: 01 450 2805
Web site: www.adventuresports.ie

National Parks and Wildlife Service
Department of Arts, Heritage,
  Gaeltacht and the Islands
'Dún Aimhirgin'
43–49 Mespil Road
Dublin 4
Tel: 01 647 3000
Fax: 01 647 3051

An Óige (Irish Youth Hostel
  Association)
61 Mountjoy Street
Dublin 1
Tel: 01 830 4555
Fax: 01 830 5808
Email: anoige@iol.ie
Web site: www.irelandyha.org

Ordnance Survey Ireland
Phoenix Park
Dublin 8
Tel: 01 820 5300
Fax: 01 820 4156
Email: custserv@osi.ie
Web site: www.irlgov.ie/osi

Stena Line
Ferry Terminal
Dún Laoghaire Harbour
Co Dublin
Tel: 01 204 7700
Fax: 01 204 7620
Web site: www.stenaline.com
Tel reservations in UK:
- 0990 707070 (travel only)
- 0990 747474 (inclusive package
  holidays)

Town and Country Homes
  Association
Head Office
Donegal Road
Ballyshannon
Co Donegal
Tel: 072 51377
Fax: 072 51207

Wicklow Mountains National Park
Glendalough
Co Wicklow
Tel: 0404 45338
Fax: 0404 45306

TOURIST BOARD, A SELECTION
OF OFFICES ABROAD AND
REGIONAL TOURISM
ORGANISATIONS
Bord Fáilte (Irish Tourist Board)
Baggot Street Bridge
Dublin 2
Tel: 01 602 4000
Fax: 01 602 4100
Email: user@irishtouristboard.ie

Irish Tourist Board
150 New Bond Street
London
England
Tel: 0171 518 0800
Fax: 0171 493 9065
(Travel enquiries Tel: 0171 493 3201)

Irish Tourist Board
Irische Fremdenverkehrszentrale
Untermainlage 7
W 6000 Frankfurt Main 1
Germany
Tel: 069 23 64 92
Fax: 069 23 46 26

Irish Tourist Board
Leidestraat 32
1017 PB Amsterdam
Holland
Tel: 020 6 22 31 01
Fax: 020 6 20 80 89

Irish Tourist Board
757 Third Avenue
New York NY 10017
USA
Tel: 212 418 0800
Fax: 212 371 9052

Irish Tourist Board
5th Level
36 Carrington Street
Sydney NSW 2000
Australia
Tel: 02 299 6177
Fax: 02 299 6323

Cork/Kerry Tourism
Tourist House
Grand Parade
Cork
Tel: 021 273251
Fax: 021 273504
Email: user@cktourism.ie

Dublin Tourism
Dublin Tourism Centre
Suffolk Street
Dublin 2
Tel: 01 605 7700
Fax: 01 605 7757
Email: marketing@dublintourism.ie
Web site: visitdublin.com

Ireland West Tourism
Áras Fáilte
Eyre Square
Galway
Tel: 091 563081
Fax: 091 565201

Midlands-East Tourism
Dublin Road
Mullingar
Co Westmeath
Tel: 044 48761
Fax: 044 40413
Email:
midlandseasttourism@eircom.net

North West Tourism
Áras Reddan
Temple Street
Sligo
Tel: 071 61201
Fax: 071 60360
Email: irelandnorthwest@eircom.net
Web site:
www.ireland-northwest.travel.ie

Tourism Division
Shannon Development
Town Centre
Shannon
Co Clare
Tel: 061 361555
Fax: 061 361903
Email: info@shannon-dev.ie

South East Tourism
41 The Quay
Waterford
Tel: 051 875823
Fax: 051 877388